Adventures In Happiness

A True Story of Travel, Change, and Adventure

To my family for their never ending support.

To my niece Holly and nephew Jack in the hope this inspires
you to live your own adventures in life.

Thank you to everyone who read, commented, and gave
feedback on this story. Especially Sally, Scooby, Julie, and
Andy Cope.

ISBN: 9781980925415

Table of Contents

Introduction

A Lion, a Donkey's Head, and Moving On in Life

"Ready, John?" shouted Cat.

"Ready," I shouted back, failing to sound convincing and, grabbing the ears of the donkeys head, I lifted it off the truck. The head felt warm, its fur thick and bristly, and as I got an idea of its weight in my hands, blood dripped over my trainers. And these were my new and expensive trainers.

The head was heavier than I expected it to be, but it was too late now, I was committed, and I looked up at the fence I hoped to clear.

On the other side paced Obi – a five-year-old male lion – and, in the moment, I couldn't help wonder if this head represented my past life. Not that I'd ever decapitated anyone, but what better way to move on from something than by feeding it to a lion!

In the distance, I heard a countdown of "three, two, one, go," and I swung the head back and launched it through the air.

At first, for a donkey's head, it flew well. But, as it clipped the top of the enclosure, I wasn't sure it would make it or fall back at my feet. But it cleared, the lion pounced, gripped the skull between his jaws, and dragged it off into the long grass.

"Did you get that?" I turned and asked the Norwegian film crew stood beside me.

"We got it," they replied and gave me a thumbs up and a smile.

I gave them a big grin in return. Because today was Monday, and I was volunteering at a big cat sanctuary in the Western Cape, South Africa. And, as my mind drifted back to the office job I'd left nine months ago, I knew my life could not have been any different.

Which was what I had wanted, and perhaps needed, from the start.

Chapter 1
Hitting the Reset Button

March 2015

The only way to create sustainable change is to reset the norm.
Andy Cope - professional trainer and author

~ Take the opportunity ~

I dropped the envelope into the post box and gave a sigh of relief. My decision was made, and it felt good. The envelope contained my acceptance of the voluntary severance offer to leave the organisation I'd worked for since I was sixteen years old.

The Human Resource team would receive the letter in a few days. I would then receive a leaving date and a goodbye presentation, someone would cut up my pass, and I would walk out the door and not come back. Twenty-one years and no more. Thanks for your service John, and goodbye.

But this decision hadn't been easy. In fact it took months of procrastinating plus a few yoga classes to settle my mind before I committed myself. Not just because I was giving up a decent wage and a final salary pension scheme, but it went against my societal conditioning of being safe, comfortable, and secure.

But none of that mattered anymore. I was ready to try something new, and it wasn't because I no longer enjoyed my work. I hoped to find value in taking a break, getting out of my comfort zone, and having chance to experience a different way of life. And this would not be possible with a few weeks holiday a year. I'd realised if I wanted to make the most of my life I needed to make things happen for myself. Because if I didn't, I would be in exactly the same place next year.

It's also worth mentioning that the opportunity to take voluntary redundancy didn't come about on its own. In fact, I'd worked hard to encourage it through negotiations with managers for a year, and it was my third application to leave before I got the chance. But why was that so important? Because it helped get me moving. Not only for the financial buffer, but it positioned me where I had no more excuses. It was now, or never.

Once HR received my letter, they told me I had four weeks left at work. It wasn't long, and as I wrapped up my projects as best I could, then said goodbye to friends, I had little chance to think about next steps.

Then, the day arrived and, as I sat waiting for my customary leaving presentation, I was a mixed bag of thoughts and emotions. I still had nothing planned, and I would leave that day. The team came in, the laptop turned on, and my leaving presentation began.

I smiled as I received a goodbye ode from my manager Julie, along with positive feedback from my other manager Steve.

Then, it was time to go. But as I walked out the glass-fronted office I'd sat in for many years, I had a massive smile on my face. And, as I discovered a few weeks later, my fist-pumping-heel-clicking-exit was captured on the security camera. I was free!

~ I was conditioned ~

As I woke for my new life of freedom, my first thought was *this feels like a holiday.* Because it coincided with the Easter break (and April Fool's day), I drove to North Wales to visit friends and family. I hoped a few days away would help me transition into my new life.

What was strange to notice was how relaxed I seemed. It was like an extended vacation. But with hindsight, I may have been in denial that I'd just quit a good job with no plan of what to do next!

As I drove, I let the thoughts of what I wanted to do run through my mind. *I could travel, maybe volunteer, perhaps even retrain.* But nothing seemed to stick. Then I remembered what a friend had said a few days ago.

"You realise you have an open book," he said. "So come on, what's the plan?"

But I didn't know 'the plan' and part of me suspected it wasn't as simple as one thing. So, I pushed the thoughts to the back of my mind and concentrated on the journey. An hour later, I arrived at the crescent-shaped bay of Rhosneigr, on the Isle of Anglesey.

Although Anglesey is far from my home in Derby, I consider it one of my favourite places in the UK to practice my passion of kitesurfing. As I looked over the sandy beach and the rugged mountainous backdrop of Snowdonia National Park, the weather seemed fine. I got the familiar excitement of being close to the ocean, able to chase the wind and the waves.

The next ten days passed by fast as the Easter holidays happened. I caught up with friends, climbed Mount Snowdon, and spent time kitesurfing. But as people returned to their daily lives, reality hit me. My time in Wales had been a fun distraction, but now I needed to decide what I wanted to do. Which is where I struggled.

For most of my life, I'd turned up, done what was asked, and rushed home to spend my pay-cheque. Now I had to make active choices which affected the rest of my life. It was proving as unnerving as it was empowering.

So, with the realisation this transition wasn't as easy as first hoped, and a head full of ideas but no firm decision, I drove back to Derby to figure out what to do next.

~ The problem is choice, the solution is easy ~

A few days had passed since I'd returned from Wales.

As I sat in my house in the Midlands, I succumbed to the fact the honeymoon period had ended. What had begun as a high culminated in a low. To make matters worse, it had begun to rain.

As I gazed through the window, I zoned out and watched beads of water forming on the glass. They left tiny trails of bubbles as they fell. And, for the first moment since I left work, I doubted what I had done.

I then jumped as I felt a pain in my thigh. "Agghh," I shouted and looked down. My cat, Mitsy, had jumped, dug her claws into my jeans, and now hung off my leg. As usual, she wanted feeding. But she had also brought me back to my self-inflicted predicament. Of course, I hadn't made the wrong decision. I just found it hard to decide what I would do next.

I wondered then if I could have been better prepared. *Perhaps,* I thought to myself. I didn't need to have life all figured out, but I needed to make my choice, and quick, because there was a risk I would end up where I started. Because that's what we sometimes do as humans. Even when we have a choice, we follow what we know, stay comfortable, and repeat our patterns.

As I leaned back in my chair and unpicked the cat's claws from my jeans, I relaxed. Then, I saw the funny side. What a paradox to have gone from no-freedom to overwhelmed by options overnight! I gave it more thought and concluded an adventure would be a great way to shake me up and give fresh perspective. So, I decided to travel. It was something I'd always talked about doing. Decision made.

I then researched countries I had an interest in and looked at South America, Europe, and Asia, but it didn't take long to confuse myself. Analysis paralysis they call it, and I was right back to where I started. So, I decided on a new approach. Just choose, trust it's the right choice, and change course if needed.

This worked, and I decided to travel Europe in a campervan. This had been a lifelong dream, and I'd bought a campervan a few years ago for this purpose. Once I had made my decision, I could think about making things happen.

Happy with where my thoughts led, I found an old map of Europe and scanned the pages for routes. I paused at Spain and noticed Tarifa - the kitesurfing capital of Europe. I'd remembered an email I'd received a few days ago from a friend, Inés, from Portugal.

The email read she planned to visit the Andalusian town in a few weeks' time and asked if I wanted to join her and her friends. What good timing.

I kept Tarifa in mind as I looked back at the map, and an idea formed. *What about across the Straits of Gibraltar to Morocco.* As much as Spain interested me, Morocco would be more of a travel experience. It was North Africa! Then I remembered discussing travels with a friend Tom I had made on my recent adventure to Wales. He'd mentioned he would be in Morocco in six weeks' time and talked about meeting.

I gave it a moment's thought and decided that was enough. I would aim for Tarifa, meet Inés, take a ferry across to Morocco, and meet Tom. Perhaps it was in my subconscious all along, but I now had 'the plan'.

~ A test to see if I was committed ~

A few days later, I took my campervan for an MOT but it failed. I was so annoyed. It had been given the all-clear a few months ago.

My plan had been to leave in a few days, but now I faced an estimated bill of two thousand pounds, plus a delay of four weeks. *The strip down, the welding, the risk of it catching fire while being fixed.* All things I didn't need to hear before embarking on an extended adventure. There was a choice to wait and change my plans, but I didn't want to take it. I guessed this to be a test of my commitment to this adventure.

Instead, I enlisted the help of my Dad to try the work myself. Over the course of the next two weeks, in-between unsettled April weather, supported by cups of tea from my mum, we did what we could. Then, I found another garage to finish the job.

As the garage completed the work, I booked a one-way ferry ticket to the north of Spain. There was no procrastination. Just a quick search for a ticket online, click buy, and done. Decision made. I would leave in six days. The campervan wasn't ready, but I had the idea I would work better under pressure. Enough time had passed since I'd left my job and I needed to get moving.

The focused approach worked. As I walked back out of the garage after the campervan retest I was smiling. My campervan passed its MOT and was now ready to go. I had cut it fine. There were only twenty-four-hours until my ferry departed, but all I had to do was pack my kites, boards, and clothes and I would be on the road.

Then I hit another disaster. With no warning, the head gasket failed on my engine and water leaked out as fast as I could pour it into the tank! Convinced that I was being told something, I limped to the garage to ask for help.

They gave me two options. Fix the problem which could cost up to a thousand pounds and take four days; or try a sealant developed for the American space programme costing thirty pounds, taking forty-five minutes. If it worked.

In my mind, I didn't have a choice. I wasn't waiting any longer, so I asked the mechanics to pour in the sealant. They did, and I stood and waited with my fingers crossed.

At first, nothing happened. But then the leak slowed, became a drip, and after thirty minutes stopped. I couldn't believe it. Thanking the mechanics I drove out the garage to a shout of "don't go far because it's only a temporary fix." But I ignored it. I would leave tomorrow regardless.

This adventure was about to begin.

Chapter 2
An Adventure into Europe and Morocco

May 2015

If happiness is the goal - and it should be, then adventure should be a priority.
Richard Branson - English business magnate

~ This is not a holiday ~

After yesterday's fiasco, I said goodbye to friends and family and made the long drive to the South Coast of the UK to board my ferry.

This was it. The start of my adventure. The leaking engine seemed to be OK, but I carried a spare bottle of the sealant which had, so far at least, cured the problem. I knew it was a risk to drive my campervan anywhere, but it was a risk I would take. *And anyway*, I told myself, *what's the worst that could happen.*

Once I'd arrived at Portsmouth, I checked my campervan was OK before boarding the twenty-four-hour Cap Finistère ferry. Everything seemed OK, and I boarded. Now I was committed. We set sail into the Atlantic Ocean and slowly moved towards the north coast of Spain.

Once the ferry settled into a steady pace, I thought back over the last six weeks. If it was anything to gauge by, I suspected I could be in for an adventure and I wondered how I'd cope. I had never travelled on my own before and now I was free to make my own decisions and mistakes. There was no-one else to rely on, and no-one else to blame.

There wasn't much to do on the ferry so I spent the time trying to learn Spanish, spoke to other travellers, and picked up a recommendation for a campsite close to the city. Until now, I'd not considered where I would sleep, but a decent night's rest made sense.

Twenty-four-hours later, once we docked into the Port of Santander, I followed the directions, and checked into a green and shaded campsite. I then tried to impress the girl behind the reception desk with my new Spanish language skills before deciding to explore the town of Santander.

It seemed a pleasant city, and I had time for a walk before the sun set. But I got locked out the campsite, had to scramble over a security fence to return to my campervan, and got into trouble with the security guards before I could rest! Unsure if excitement or nerves bothered me, sleep didn't come easy that first night.

The following morning, after discussing ideas with travellers on site, I decided to drive to the Picos de Europa mountains. They were not far. Perhaps an hour away, and keen to get straight to travelling I left the campsite early and drove west along the coast road.

The warm weather and easy drive served as a nice introduction to life in Spain. After an hour, I turned south and made my way inland until the sights of the tall, grey, mountains came into view. I found an alpine village called Potés, and deciding to base myself, parked my campervan, and explored.

Then, a strange thing happened.

As I walked the narrow cobbled streets and explored the medieval style town, I kept seeing the same girl wherever I went. This went on for an hour until, intrigued and distracted by what kept happening, I bumped into her by chance outside a coffee shop. We both saw the funny side of what seemed a predestined meet and agreed to sit and share a drink.

We got on well. She told me her name was Olga, that she was an English teacher from Russia, and nicknamed herself

'The Curious Russian Fox' for her curious nature and love of travel.

Over the next few hours, she told me about life in Saint Petersburg and I talked about my recent changes and current plans. Conversations continued until she stopped and asked me if I knew what I was doing. Confused, I put this down to a language barrier. Of course I knew what I was doing, and I asked her to explain.

"Well," she said, "you keep saying this is a holiday. But this is more. From what you've told me, you are following your own path, and your own purpose."

Laughing, I replied "In that case, I know what my purpose is. To travel. At least for now."

"OK," she continued, "why do you keep calling it a holiday if you are certain it to be more." She fixed her eyes on me and stared, waiting for my answer.

I stuttered because she was right. I was still thinking of this adventure as an extended holiday. She must have sensed my unease because she let it drop. The conversation then switched to something else, and soon after she said she had to leave.

Because she was heading in the same direction as me, I offered her a lift.

"No, it's fine," she told me. "I'd better not. I must return to my husband. He is sleeping. I am on my honeymoon and came for a walk. But remember what I said, it might be important."

With that, she smiled, and with a knowing glint in her eyes, turned her back on me and walked away.

~ Because someday can be today ~

After spending the night in Potés, I took an early cable car up the mountain peaks.

I was the first to the top and stood, ankle deep in snow and stared up at the sheer faces of the peaks in complete silence. Until now, I didn't appreciate this part of Spain to be so beautiful.

Keen to explore whilst up high, I followed what looked like a well-trodden path which cut across the foot of a mountain. I walked for thirty minutes but the snow proved too deep. Instead, I turned around, and found a different path that wound down a valley.

As I walked, the area seemed very peaceful and green, and I didn't see another soul for hours until I noticed an old man stood at a crossroad. He looked lost, and walking over to him I asked if he was OK.

He introduced himself as John, said he was walking on his own, and suggested we share the walk. I agreed, and together we kept moving.

John told me he came from Australia, but lived most of his life in Spain working as an English teacher. While he had interesting stories to tell, he spoke with such enthusiasm for the beauty of the Spanish cities of Salamanca, Madrid, and Cordoba, he convinced me I should see them for myself someday.

Then, as we kept walking, something dawned on me. Someday could be today. Why did I have to wait until next week, next month, or next year to do the things I wanted? I was free. This was my time.

With that in mind, once we had returned to the village where I started my day, I thanked him for his ideas, left the mountains, and began the four hundred kilometre drive south towards Salamanca.

- - - - - - - - - - - -

After spending the night in a lorry carpark, I arrived at the UNESCO city just before lunchtime.

It looked an interesting place, and parking my campervan on the outskirts, I rode my pushbike into the centre and, for the next few days, explored the Plaza's, gardens, and restaurants.

It was nice, with lots of impressive buildings, academics, coffee shops, and tourists. But for the first time since starting this adventure, a sense of loneliness washed over me.

I hadn't expected this, but it wasn't a problem, I just shifted my thinking to appreciate it was healthy to solo travel. Then, a man propositioned me as I walked the busy squares! I was flattered, but it wasn't quite what I expected, and taking that as my cue to leave, I returned to my campervan, and drove five hundred kilometres south towards Cordoba.

I arrived late the same evening, parked my campervan in the centre of the city, and went to explore.

I liked it straight away. Because of its history of invasion by the Moorish armies, it had more of an Islamic style than Salamanca. For whatever reason, something drew me in, and I then spent the next two days exploring the old Mosque-Cathedral, irregular streets of the Jewish quarter, and backpacker style bars.

I loved the vibrant energy and had a good time, but it also proved to be hot. A heat wave had engulfed this part of Spain and the temperature reached the forties. After waking to the smell of sour milk one morning because my fridge had broken, I admitted defeat.

The cities had been fun, but it was time to get to the coast. It was time to get to Tarifa.

~ Adapting to life in Tarifa ~

As I followed the mountain roads south through the Andalusian countryside, the small town of Tarifa came into view. Once a sleepy fishing village, now one of the most popular locations in Europe for wind and water sports.

This also marked the southernmost point of Continental Europe. Any farther south I would be in Africa. I had moved fast for the past week, but I now planned to stay still, kitesurf and relax.

I arrived as the sun set into the ocean, emailed my friend to meet tomorrow, and slept.

The following morning, I caught up with Inés and met a group from Portugal, Italy, and Canada. They were all fun people, and in true Tarifa style we agreed to go kitesurfing.

The conditions on the water were perfect. After the past week of travelling, I appreciated getting to the beach, setting up equipment, and having the chance to kitesurf in the strong winds. Once kitesurfing finished, drinks in town followed which concluded with a six am finish, two hours sleep, and a parking ticket stuck to my campervan window!

It was a fun start to my time in Tarifa. But, by the third day of the same, even though I'd had a good time, I started to think I wanted more from this adventure than just partying.

Then, something happened which confirmed my thoughts.

Inés and her friends had returned to their daily lives, and I'd met another group of people from the UK. They were friendly and invited me to a party one evening on the outskirts of town. I decided to go.

The night started well.

There was good music, flowing drinks, and friendly people, and everyone seemed to have a good time until one of the group, Soos, approached me late on, looking worried.

"John," she said, "have you seen Caroline?"

"Not for the last hour," I said. "Why, what's up?"

"She was acting strange. I think she drank too much, and now she's disappeared. Will you help me look for her?"

I agreed and we spent the next three hours combing the streets and eventually found her sheltering under a bus stop with no recollection of how she got there! She was upset but OK, and we put this down to a lesson learned, but I decided then it was time to make a change.

- - - - - - - - - - - -

The next day, I said goodbye to my friends and went to find a quiet spot on the edge of town. I wanted time on my own to think what to do next.

It didn't take long to find a quiet beach to free camp, and once I had settled into my new place, I slowed myself down.

Then, everything hit me at once. The build-up to leaving work, the trouble with my campervan, the first week travelling, and now the lack of sleep and head splitting hangover. I felt terrible!

For the next few days, I tried running on the beach and focused on my kitesurfing, but it didn't seem to help. Even though I enjoyed the campervan life, I started to think I'd made some bad choices because I wasn't that happy.

I decided then to cut myself some slack. I'd only left work six weeks ago, and I'd been running at full speed for years. It was understandable to find the transition strange. I needed to accept it would take time to adjust. I needed to keep busy, but busy with the right things. So I arranged to meet with a girl I'd spoken to on a night out.

Her name was Virginia, and she was from Ceuta, an autonomous Spanish city joined to Morocco but lived in Tarifa. She was typical of the girls of Andalusia, with long flowing dark hair and eyes that hinted of the Moorish conquests. But there was a small problem. She spoke less English than I spoke Spanish.

But I need not have worried. The first evening we met was strange, but as we spent time together, we found the language barrier added a level of fun. With the help of a mobile phone translator, we ate in restaurants, explored the area, and relaxed at the beach.

Over the next few days, she taught me Spanish as I told her about my changes and plans, and we became friends. Other than coming close to being arrested following a moonlit swim, time with her turned out to be what I needed.

- - - - - - - - - - - -

As the week passed, I knew I'd begun to adjust to my new life.

Fun times with my friend had helped, as had exploring the old town and kitesurfing, but I wondered if I should do something else. After so many years working, I needed to channel my mental energy. I wanted a purpose other than sitting on a beach or kitesurfing.

So, I decided to create a blog. Not only did I want to capture my journey, I hoped it would be the perfect way to share idiosyncrasies of life on the road.

I found a quiet coffee shop, connected to the internet, and made a start.

It went well. I enjoyed the writing and feedback from friends told me "I brightened their dull day at work with stories of my adventures." But I found the writing had an unexpected effect. It was cathartic. As I wrote, it put recent changes into perspective. And then I started to think about what to do next.

In the distance, across the narrow Straits of Gibraltar, I could see Africa. In fact, if I stood at one of the high vantage points in town, I could see the flickering lights of Tangier. I was still drawn to an adventure on another continent.

Then, I received an email from Tom, my friend from Wales. The timing was perfect. The email read he had arrived at the Moroccan coastal city of Essaouira and asked me to join him.

I considered my options. I had been in Tarifa three weeks. If I took the ferry across the water and tackled the drive south, I would be there in two days. We would kitesurf together, and when he returned to the UK, I would be in a position to travel Morocco on my own.

This is tempting I thought. But I hesitated. Even though I was drawn to another continent, everyone I spoke to about Morocco warned me how dangerous it was. I could just stay here and enjoy Tarifa. But I snapped out of it. Where would be the fun and adventure in staying safe? If I didn't try, I would never know. I decided to leave the next day.

That night, I said goodbye to my friend Virginia and got ready for Morocco.

"Please, be careful," she told me as I made to leave. "Morocco is not Europe. Tangier I do not like. This is not a good place. Stay safe."

But I'm not sure I listened. This time tomorrow, I would stand on a different continent.

~ Trouble in Tangier ~

It was easy to catch a ferry from Tarifa across the Straits of Gibraltar to Morocco, but forty five minutes later, as the boat pulled into the port city of Tangier, I stood on a very different continent. Tangier looked, like most port towns and cities, that it had an element of danger to it.

As I cleared customs with the help of a local fixer, I made for a dockside cabin to buy insurance. To drive around a country with as bad a reputation as Morocco for traffic accidents, without insurance, would be foolish. I knew, through an email conversation with the Moroccan driving agency, that I could arrange it at the port upon arrival.

As I got close to the cabin, I saw a sign read *closed*. By the looks of how quiet it was, it would not open soon. *Great*, I thought to myself. *Now what*. I didn't fancy waiting around.

Then, out of the corner of my eye, I noticed a man approaching me. As he got close, he smiled a toothless grin and told me in bad English the office was shut. I said nothing, but he stood there weighing me up, pulled an old mobile phone from his pocket, and made a call.

Within minutes, a car pulled up and another man stepped out. He looked younger. About thirty.

"Welcome to my country," he said, opening his arms wide as if to emphasise his point. "I am Karim, how can I help you?"

I guessed things happened fast here, but I ignored his offer, and asked if the office here would open soon.

"Oh no," he said, smiling an even broader smile. "Today, the office is closed. Today is Friday. The holy day. If you want insurance, you must come with me and Abdul into Tangier."

Abdul, I assumed, was his toothless sidekick, and I considered my options. Insurance was a necessity. I didn't want to navigate Tangier on my own, these two didn't look intimidating, so I agreed. *And anyway*, I thought, as we all got in my campervan together, *what's the worst that can happen.*

- - - - - - - - - - - -

The city was crazy!

Traffic came from all directions, and I needed to focus to not hit someone or something. Men walked down the streets holding hands. Women walked with their faces covered. And groups of people sat in circles smoking and sharing large glass pipes.

As we got further into the centre of the madness, Karim told me to stop outside an insurance broker. I did, and he ran in and organised what I needed.

It seemed straightforward enough, cost about five hundred Dirham, or eighty euros, and once arranged, as a way of celebrating, he suggested we sit and have a drink. We found a roadside restaurant, took a seat and ordered traditional hot sweet mint tea.

Then, I relaxed. I couldn't believe I was sitting in the middle of Tangier watching the pace of the city. But I was pleased. I had taken a chance and got what I'd needed. Even though I knew it would cost me for their help, I doubted it would be much.

After thirty minutes of sitting people watching, Karim turned to face me and asked my plans. I told him I would drive towards Rabat.

"OK," he said jumping from his seat. "Let's go. I'll show you the way, but one last thing. Whatever you do, do not pick up any strangers. Remember we are not in Europe John. This is North Africa. Trust no-one. And I mean no-one."

I wasn't sure what to think but kept my mouth shut. We got in my campervan and drove away from the city in silence.

Thirty minutes into the drive, Karim told me to pull to the side of the road. I did, and he stepped out of my campervan and walked round to my door. Abdul, who had sat in the rear, moved to the front, and as Karim leaned in through my window and smiled, I guessed what was coming.

"Now you must pay him," he gestured toward Abdul.

Having prepared a figure in mind I turned to offer Abdul money but he cut me off mid-sentence and demanded 1500 Dirham. That converted to almost €250. It was too much. Instead, I offered him 500 Dirham and showed him the money. He stared at me, snatched the notes from my hands, and threw them in my face.

"You give me more," he demanded.

This wasn't working out as expected, and unsure what else to do and panicking, I started my campervan and drove up the road leaving Karim standing at the side of the road. It was a smart move. As I checked my mirror, I saw him shaking his head in disbelief and walking away. Now I just had to deal with Abdul.

I slowed down, pulled my campervan to the side of the road, stopped, and offered him the money again. He was fuming with rage. I tried to stay calm, but he grabbed the notes, threw them back at me, and demanded more.

Then I lost my cool. Acting on nothing but instinct, I undid his seat belt with one hand, opened his door with the other, dug my shoulder into his ribs, and forced him from my campervan with a shove.

"MORE MONEY YOU FUCK," he screamed at me as he rolled backwards into the road. I had pushed a fist full of notes into his hand as he fell, but he was out, and I was gone.

~ The travelling helps to adjust ~

As I saw a service station, I pulled my campervan in and stopped. My heart pounded, and I dripped in sweat. For a second I thought about taking a ferry back to Spain.

Embarrassed, I got myself together. I was here to travel. I couldn't give in at the first thing which proved hard. Putting it down to experience, I continued two hundred kilometres south towards Rabat.

When I arrived three hours later, I was glad to find the city far removed from Tangier. Parking my campervan at a modern looking centre, I got help from a girl behind the counter of a shop to set up a SIM card on my phone. She also offered advice on where to go in the country. Thankfully, she wanted nothing in return.

I soon left the modern city behind and followed the coast road further south and stopped at a campsite on the edge of the Atlantic Ocean near Casablanca. There wasn't much here. Just a dusty street and a small shop serving passing travellers but it was OK for a night.

- - - - - - - - - - - -

The following morning, I continued the four hundred kilometre drive south to Essaouira.

As I got deeper into the country, I saw how different life compared to Europe. The dusty streets were full with people, chickens, and cars sharing the same space. As if to emphasise the difference, as I drove through a village, just before I joined a well-developed motorway, I noticed a body – a young man lying on his back at an unnatural angle. Next to him parked a damaged car and stood a crowd of people. No-one helped. I assumed he was already dead.

After leaving the dusty roads, I re-joined the motorway, continued through Marrakech, turned west, and arrived three hours later at the port city of Essaouira.

I quickly found a place to stay, met with Tom, and found the summer trade winds that make the beach popular for kitesurfing blowing strong. After a quick hello, it was straight onto the water for a kitesurfing session.

We both needed it. Tom was nursing a hangover, and after the past few days of travelling, I was ready to have the stresses washed off by the cold Atlantic Ocean. The kitesurfing was good as we spent a few hours chasing across the waves, but I soon tired and arranged to meet with Tom again tomorrow.

After packing my equipment away, I returned to my campervan to sleep.

- - - - - - - - - - - -

The next morning, I explored what presented itself as an interesting place to be. And not only to kitesurf.

There was a mix of Berber, Arabian, and European cultures, and the town was surrounded by a raw and natural beauty. I spoke to other travellers, picked up ideas for places to visit, and relaxed into the city.

Then, I realised today was the first of June. The day marked a milestone for me. Two months had passed since I'd left work, and this was now the longest I'd lived without structure since I'd started school, aged four.

As I met up with Tom later that day to go kitesurfing, I mentioned this to him. He was curious why I believed it was significant.

"I think it explains why it's taken a while to adjust into my new life," I told him. "I'm sure I liked things to be safe and certain, and most of what I'm doing now is the opposite!"

He laughed. "Yeah, you're probably right," he said. "From a life of a structured routine to complete freedom overnight. It's enough to unsettle anyone."

The conversation then shifted onto something else and we got ready to go kitesurfing. But, in the back of my mind, I knew the positives these changes would bring. Not only was I living free and travelling, I was, in some ways, working through my conditioning.

I wondered then, just for a moment, what life would have been like if I'd waited any longer to make a change. Would I have been happy? I didn't know, but one thing was for certain. To be following my own path was empowering.

- - - - - - - - - - - -

A few days later, Tom returned to the UK, and I was on my own again.

I had enjoyed the company, so I left behind the comfort of my campervan, checked into a busy hostel which overlooked the old medina, and met a mix of other travellers. There were all ten years younger than me, but it didn't matter and, from the hostel, I took the chance to explore the city walls.

I found the souk and spent a morning getting lost in the busy streets, then explored the working harbour where I bought fish straight from a boat and had it cooked in front of me at a local market. I was also encouraged to go to a Senegalese music event as part of the Moroccan Woodstock festival and danced to the best house music I had heard for a long time!

But, after two more days, I decided to move on. The time in the hostel had been a nice change from living in my campervan, but eight days had passed since I'd arrived at Essaouira and I was keen to get moving.

I knew where to go, but wanted advice, and went to speak to the owner of a kitesurfing school I'd met.

His name was Azdoul, and he soon convinced me my idea was sound. I had told him I'd thought about visiting the High Atlas Mountains and he had said one thing:

"They would be good for me."

That was all I needed to hear, and the next day I left Essaouira behind, happy I had come here.

~ The joy is in the climb ~

Not long after leaving Essaouira, a policeman stopped me for speeding. I didn't think it possible for my campervan to go so fast but I paid my fine, continued east through Sidi Mokhtar, and slept the night at the foot of a dusty village near Chichaoua.

After an early start the next day, I followed the road south and arrived at the outskirts of Imlil, the small village used as a base for tackling the High Atlas Mountains, before lunchtime. It had been a long drive to get here from Essaouira. Almost two hundred and fifty kilometres.

As I entered the village, I noticed a car following me which then flashed its lights and showed I should pull over and stop. Thinking there might be something wrong with my campervan, I did, but kept my engine running.

A man then stepped out of the car and ambled towards me. He was dressed in a long white Djellaba – a loose-fitting robe with full-length sleeves. As he got close to my window, he introduced himself as Mohammad and explained he was a local businessman. I said nothing.

He then explained he could organise a trek in the mountain if I was interested. *This is great timing*, I thought to myself, but my mind cast back to Tangier. Could this be a hustle, or an opportune meet to organise something I wanted?

I decided the latter. I didn't want to tarnish my adventure with a bad experience. He seemed to offer what I wanted, so I agreed to follow him through the village to his home and business.

When I arrived at his home, I saw his business was a legitimate set-up. Also staying here were a squadron of British soldiers on exchange with the Moroccan army. Straight away, they welcomed me into their group and gave me advice on things to do in the area.

"Trek up to Jbel Toubkal," they suggested. "It's the highest mountain in North Africa. Then explore the local villages and other mountain peaks. But watch out for Mohammed. He's a cut-throat businessman."

Thanking them for the advice, I organised a guided trek to the summit of the highest peak and took myself to bed. But not before one of the Moroccan soldiers gave me a present for my journey. A camelback to store water in when hiking.

I was quite humbled. He wanted nothing in return.

- - - - - - - - - - - -

The trek began early the following morning when my young but experienced guide Azdoul collected me.

After brief introductions, we began our walk and climbed from an altitude of 1500 metres through a Berber village and up the side of a rocky valley.

It was a good hike. Azdoul was friendly and good company. Along the way we passed men selling mint teas, pack mules carrying heavy loads, other climbers, and another guide carrying a live chicken strung up by its feet.

After four hours, we came to our overnight stop – the Refuge du Toubkal at a height of 3200 metres. The usual thing was to rest, sleep, and summit at first light, but my guide had other ideas.

"You're looking strong John," he told me. "We should continue. That way no crowds. No people. We'll be on our own at the top."

I paused for a moment and considered what he'd said. To try for the summit without crowds appealed. I felt strong enough, Azdoul seemed to think there was time, so I agreed, and we continued.

I was grateful for Azdoul. He was an excellent guide, but, after a few hours of cutting a path through scattered rocks and melting snow fields, I questioned my decision to continue without a break. I had a pounding headache and the higher I climbed, the worse it became. It was the onset of altitude sickness. I needed to slow down or I wouldn't make it to the top.

I was just thinking *I should have given myself a chance to acclimatise to the altitude* when I saw a man stumbling down the mountain towards us. He was out of breath and supported by two guides.

"What are you doing," he told me in a French accent, whilst flapping his arms in a panic. "It's too late, the climb is too hard, you won't get to the top."

This wasn't what I needed to hear, and I turned to Azdoul to check we had time to summit, even at a much slower pace.

"Yes, we have plenty," he told me, "but we must keep moving. It is getting late."

So I did my best to ignore the pessimism and headache, pushed on and up, and slowly moved along what seemed an endless rocky slope.

An hour later, we came to the summit ridge. Then, I saw the summit itself in the distance and, motivated by the end in sight, with a final push, thirty minutes later we reached the top.

And what a view! In every direction rugged mountain peaks stretched back to the line of the horizon. They were dusty orange and the sense of space took my breath away.

Azdoul then turned to face me, smiled, congratulated me, and asked how I was feeling.

"Amazing," I told him, and I meant it. For the moment, my headache had gone and my pain forgotten. There was no-one else at this height of 4167 meters, and that made us the highest men in North Africa!

We took a seat and took in the views. It was incredible, and so quiet, but as we sat, I realised something. It had been a tough hike to get here, but without the effort it wouldn't be half as impressive as it seemed. Which meant the joy had been in the climb. I knew it a cliché, but I couldn't help but think that counted for a lot of things in life.

Fifteen minutes later, as the sun dipped below the peaks of the mountains, and shadows cast across the steep slopes, Azdoul suggested we leave. I agreed, and we inched our way back down the slopes.

Two hours later we were back at the refuge. But the only joy I got from this was a freezing cold shower. We were so late back there was no hot water left, plus I'd forgotten my towel.

~ Highs, lows, and internal conflicts of life on the road ~

The mountains captured me so much I extended my stay with Mohammad, and spent three days exploring waterfalls, Berber villages, and mountain valleys.

I met and spoke with the locals and watched children play in the streets, and even saw a hen party equivalent of a Berber wedding, as the bride and entourage danced, drummed, and sang through people's homes.

Life worked for me here. The landscape, people, the simplicity. The villagers didn't have much, but they appeared happy, and this got me thinking about my material possessions at home. Did they make me happy. Or did they tie me to what I didn't need.

Then, even though I could have stayed longer, but not before I'd eaten dinner at the most expensive hotel in town with an attractive Siberian girl I'd met while hiking, I said goodbye to people I'd met.

While it was sad to leave, I knew it was time to move on, but as I drove out of the village and joined the main roads north, which led me towards Marrakesh, I remembered what Azdoul from Essaouira had said over a week ago. He had been right. Time here had been good for me.

- - - - - - - - - - - -

Three hours later, I hit Marrakesh.

A few weeks ago, I had little interest in what I expected to be a crazy city. But it was close, and I wanted to check what the fuss was about.

I soon found a campsite near to the centre, checked in, relaxed, made a plan for the day, and rode my pushbike straight into the madness.

It was great! What finer way to see the vibrant pace of a city than riding a pushbike through the middle – cars mixed with horse and carts, motorbikes flew past carrying four people, and lorries overladen with goods forced everyone else out the way.

It was crazy, but it worked.

As I arrived at the old city walls, I stopped at the famous Jamaa el Fna square, locked up my pushbike, and explored.

But it was disappointing. Within minutes I saw street vendors hustling with monkeys on chains, snake charmers demanding money, and semi-naked tourists wandering the streets. From the raw and natural beauty of the mountains to this seemed a bad choice, and I left the square to explore the bazaars which form part of the medina, hoping for a saving grace – that the sunset would bring a different atmosphere.

When I returned, it had. The square had come alive with food stalls, music, smoke, and smells. While it still seemed touristy, there was life and energy, and it became a fun place to spend hours sampling the food and street entertainment before I returned to my campervan later that night, happy with my days adventure.

But my day wasn't finished. As I got changed to sleep, a man's face appeared out of the darkness and pressed against my campervan window. Panicked, I flung the door open to confront my German campervan neighbour.

"What the hell are you doing?" I demanded.

"Sorry, sorry," he muttered, "I wanted to make sure you were back safe. The roads here are very dangerous, but OK, you're here. Goodnight."

I thanked him for his concern, slid the door shut, and even though I'm sure he was genuine, locked the catch.

- - - - - - - - - - - -

The next day, after swapping a T-shirt with a local man who passed through the campsite for a camel sticker as a reminder of my stay, I said goodbye to Marrakesh, and drove farther east inland.

I didn't have a destination in mind and my day started well, but as the kilometres passed, something didn't feel right. I was undecided with what I wanted to do. After an hour, I pulled over, opened out a giant map of Morocco, laid it on my knees, and pondered. But it didn't help. I just became more indecisive. So much so, I wasted the whole afternoon not doing anything, and spent the night sleeping by the side of the road, not having gone anywhere!

After waking early the next day, I phoned home to speak to someone I knew. As I explained my indecisions my family laughed, but understood it's useful to bounce ideas off other people. They also reminded me I needed to choose. So, I stuck with travelling and continued driving east to Ouarzazate to visit the UNESCO protected Kasbah Taouritt.

After two hours, I arrived, parked my campervan, and explored. It was interesting to see but after an hour of viewing what had been a film set for Gladiator and Star Wars, I returned to my campervan to find someone had put a deep scratch across the bonnet.

I cursed my luck. Was I giving out such bad vibes I attracted them in return? Or was something else happening? It was hard to pinpoint why, but I had noticed tension in the air as I drove, and seen fights break out at some market stalls I'd passed today. I put it down to the heat and shrugged it off, got in my campervan and continued to drive.

As I did, my thoughts fell into place. It didn't matter what I did because it was all a good choice. I was following what I wanted by moving and travelling, and I needed to let the self-created-conflict go.

Then, as I kept driving, something bizarre happened. Yesterday, in amongst all my indecision, I had been trying to find a campsite said *to be a haven from the dusty Moroccan roads*. I'd had no luck, but now, right in front of me stood the entrance, and I had driven down this road four times yesterday.

How I missed this, I'm not sure. But perhaps I had been so wrapped up in my thoughts, so wrapped up in my mind, I had not seen what was right in front of me all along.

~ Some experiences are better shared ~

The next morning, after sleeping soundly at the campsite that really was a haven from the dusty Moroccan roads, and now with a clear plan, I drove east through the Vallee du Dades before continuing towards Merzouga.

I wanted to visit one of only two Erg Chebbi's in Morocco. I'd been told these wind formed sand dunes were a must see, and after trepidation in making the four hundred kilometre drive, I arrived late afternoon.

As I checked my sat nav, I realised I was now on the border with Algeria, 3500 kilometres from home. There wasn't much here. Camels, the town of Merzouga in the distance, and the desert – a pale strip of orange that ran the line of the horizon. It looked an unnatural backdrop to the dusty town.

Once I got my bearings of the area, I passed the offer of accommodation from a tout who followed me on his motorbike, found a campsite, and checked in. We were close to the sand dunes. The sun was setting, but I asked the owner if I had time to explore the desert before it became dark.

"If you are quick," he told me.

Thanking him, I avoided packs of wild dogs and made my way out of the campsite, across a rocky path, and into the dunes.

As I came close, I saw they were more orange than any sand I'd seen before, but fine underfoot and easy to walk on, and I aimed straight for the highest collection. I didn't stop moving until I reached the top, and when I got there, I found a place to sit and relaxed. It was very isolated. The town's lights flickered in the distance, but I was surrounded by an ocean of sand. It was a perfect place to catch my thoughts and reflect on the past few weeks.

There had been a few trials, but today, as seemed the norm with travelling, it felt worth it. One day good, the next not, and I wondered why today was different. Perhaps it was the desert which made everything else seem insignificant. Or

I was getting used to how it could be when you followed your own path.

Either way, as I watched the sun set and saw shadows dance across the dunes, I knew I was doing OK on this adventure of mine, and happy to have stopped in the desert, I made my way back to the campsite, and slept.

- - - - - - - - - - - -

For the next two days, I did little except relax. After the recent adventures it was nice to rest, but once I had, I realised I wanted to spend time with other people. The owner of the campsite had mentioned a guided camel safari through the desert.

Until now, I'd avoided something so touristy, but I decided to try, and as I made my way to meet a group of other travellers on the tour, I suspected I was in for a fun time.

Once the group convened, we mounted camels and rode deep into the desert and, two hours later, arrived at a semi-permanent and basic camp.

As we settled into our base, our guides became our cooks and the rest of us got to know each other. They were decent people. Three long-term travellers from Argentina, and a couple from Slovenia.

The evening passed as we swapped travel stories and ideas of new places to go, and once we'd watched another sunset and eaten a delicious Tagine cooked meal, we lay down on the floor to watch for shooting stars. Uninhibited by light pollution under the clear desert sky, it didn't take long.

And then, our peace was shattered by a scream! Matias, one of the group, had jumped up and stood clutching his hand.

"Shit, shit, shit," he shouted. "Something's bitten me." He looked in pain.

We scanned the floor, saw nothing, but checked his hand. We saw marks on his fingers and they looked swollen. He panicked. The guides asked what was wrong and quickly understood what had happened. A scorpion.

Unfazed, they picked up a gas cylinder, pressed Matias's hand to the nozzle, and turned on the gas. Within moments the escaping gas cooled the sting, and as his pain eased, he calmed. Only now did we laugh. Stung by a scorpion in the desert, miles from anywhere.

I heard one of the other group say something to Matias in Spanish, and they both laughed.

"What's that," I asked, and both laughing they told me it translated as "thanks for taking one for the team."

"That's funny," I replied. "I was thinking the very same thing."

- - - - - - - - - - - -

The next day, tired from lack of sleep but happy with our mini adventure, we returned to our own camps, said farewell, and went our separate ways. It had been a great experience, and I was eager to move again.

After speaking to my host at the campsite, I knew which route to take north. My first planned stop was Azrou, four hundred kilometres from here. But he also made sure I knew which areas to avoid because of drug plantations that cover the country.

Thanking my host, I said goodbye and drove out of the campsite. But, before I had gone far, I remembered something I'd wanted to do. I stopped my campervan next to a road sign written in Arabic and, standing in front, took a picture of myself, my campervan, and the bottle of sealant used by the garage that had proven more than a temporary fix.

This was as far south as I would go for now and I couldn't believe a thirty pound bottle of sealant had saved my adventure!

~ Challenges and experiences ~

I spent the next few days driving north through an ever-changing landscape. From dusty plains and poor villages, to green fertile valleys and back into the mountains again.

I smiled at an old man as he chugged past on his tractor and tipped his hat at me, before spending the night in the small town of Azrou which was more Swiss than Moroccan in style.

I also had the chance to explore the untouristy Imperial city of Meknes where I amazed at the traditional meat and fish markets, and laughed at a young man who got his truck stuck in the narrow streets of the medina. He wasn't bothered. He just unloaded his goods, left his truck, and carried on about his day!

By the third day of driving, I arrived at Chefchaouen, on the edge of the Rif mountains, as the sun set on another Moroccan evening.

The old city, known as the blue pearl of Morocco, famous for its hued blue-washed buildings, looked like a nice place to spend a few days and I was determined to finish my Moroccan adventure on a high.

I found a campsite that overlooked the medina, checked in, and relaxed.

- - - - - - - - - - - -

The following morning, I explored and soon settled into the slow pace of life.

The buildings were striking in their colours, and the cobbled streets full of old leather workshops and other interesting shops. But I was also here for something else.

The highest mountain in the area was close, and I fancied my chances at another summit attempt. After a conversation with a local who worked at the campsite who reassured me it was an easy climb, I went to find my way to the summit of Jebel El-Kelaa.

The hike got off to a good start, but three hours in, after realising this part of Morocco was famous for growing most of the countries marijuana, I was lost.

It wasn't a big problem. I had food, water, and dope if I wanted it, but as I scrambled across granite rocks and pushed my way through thick bush to find a path to the top, I wished I had used a guide. Then, as I was distracted by my thoughts, I slipped and fell a few meters.

There was a second of nothing, then the pain hit. For a moment I didn't dare move. I was certain I'd broken a rib, but I had been lucky. I'd fallen on rocks but my rucksack cushioned the fall. I rolled over, found a deep cut on my back, but nothing broken.

Then, the stupidity of trying to force my way to the top dawned on me, and defeated, I turned around and headed back into the city.

- - - - - - - - - - - -

The following day was my final in Morocco and I spent the evening in the main Uta el-Hammam square as the sun set and marked the end of the days fasting.

My time here coincided with Ramadan, which I had expected to be a hindrance to travelling, but found it had brought me closer to what had become more important than ticking sights off a list – a real look at the country I'd travelled.

As I walked through the square, savouring my last night, a group of men sitting around a large pan of food called me. I expected they wanted to sell me something, but I misunderstood.

As I got close, someone found a stool, asked me to sit, and passed me a piece of fresh bread. I glanced at the pan, saw it to be full of sardines cooking in tomato sauce and, as they invited me to eat, I realised what was happening. They were breaking their fast. Embarrassed by my judgement, I joined them and did my best to answer questions about who I was and what I thought of Morocco.

I realised then how much the country had grown on me. Even though my time had been a challenging month, I'd fallen for the old cities and their atmospheres, the people, mountains, beaches, and the ever-changing landscape. I'd even become accustomed to the sound of the call to prayer.

There had been moments when returning to Spain seemed the better idea, but I was glad to have stuck with it. It was hard to pinpoint why, but after all this time, it felt like my adventure was coming together.

~ Testing toward ways that work ~

The next day, I caught the ferry for Spain, left Morocco behind, and forty-five minutes later I was back in Tarifa.

It looked the same as before, but something felt different. Then, I realised that might have been me. I'd returned more confident, and I knew my time had been a worthwhile month of travelling. Much more in line with what I'd hoped and envisaged an adventure to be about.

As I cleared Spanish customs, I arranged to meet a friend Bella, from Australia. She had also arrived at Tarifa and had messaged whilst I'd travelled Morocco to gauge my interest in doing work with her. I was looking for my new focus so met her at one of the beach bars that line the coast to find out more information.

The last time I'd seen Bella was in South Africa on holiday. It was strange to see her here in Tarifa, made even more surprising by the contrast of Morroco. But, as we shared a pizza and beer, I found out she needed someone to research topics to support a story she was writing on fighting depression.

It was quite a wide subject but because the topics touched on some the things I'd become interested in with my lifestyle changes, it caught my attention. I thought about it for a moment and said yes.

I hated to admit it but my Moroccan adventure was over, and it was straight back to work!

- - - - - - - - - - - -

I soon adjusted back into Tarifa lifestyle and my days became a mix of early starts, internet research, and afternoon kitesurfing sessions.

Even though I missed Morocco, I was happy with a new focus, made a strong start on the work, and a week soon passed.

Life here was good, but in-between working I slipped into habits of staying up late, drinking, dancing and partying. Of course, a little party hurt nobody, and it became a fun time sweet-talking bouncers to gain entry to a club to impress a Dutch sailor called Suzanne who I'd met. But, as I returned to my campervan at five am, three days in a row, I knew this wasn't the best approach to getting work done.

I wanted to take consistent steps towards a healthier life but I needed something to focus on. Then, I remembered a triathlon in the UK I'd entered at the start of the year. It would take place in September. It was now July. I had put the event to one side while travelling, but perhaps I could fit in the training?

I decided this could be a new challenge. Something to run in parallel with my travelling. Even though I could run quite well, I considered myself average on a bike, and a very weak swimmer. Plus, at an Olympic distance, the triathlon would be out my comfort zone. I just needed a kick-start to my training, and by chance, I met Danni.

She managed a health and juice bar at one of the kitesurfing beaches, but also ran detox programmes. During a conversation about healthy lifestyle one afternoon, I mentioned I wanted to train, and she said she could help with one of her body reset programme.

"What's that all about?" I asked.

"Simple," she said. "I'll make you five fruit or green juices each day along with one almond milk. Start your day with warm lemon juice, drink the juices every two hours throughout the day, and finish with the milk. It will flush you out and reset your body ready to train."

"How long do I have to follow it for?"

"Start with three days and see how you get on. You will know it's working when you stop getting headaches from caffeine withdrawal and your poo turns green!"

I was dubious but agreed. I had nothing to lose and wanted a head-start with my training. So, for the next three days, as promised, Danni delivered her fresh juices, and I stuck to her instructions.

It didn't take long to have an effect. By the end of the first day, I suffered headaches from caffeine withdrawal, sugar cravings by the second day, and hunger pains by the third. But, by the end of day three, because it had such an effect and I was starting to feel good, I extended to a full seven days.

The results astounded me. Over the next four days, I lost weight, kicked any interest in sugar, alcohol, and caffeine, and my skin glowed. And, motivated by what happened, I began to run and swim, and committed to changing how I ate.

Then, the real benefits came. I slept better, had more energy and people commented "I looked healthy," and I felt great. In fact, I felt the best I had since I'd left work and started to travel.

~ Content with life on the road ~

Another week in Tarifa passed. I'd completed my research work, my fitness training was going well, and I began to think *what's next*.

As much fun as it had become kitesurfing, spending time with friends, and admiring the healthy looking people on the beaches, I knew travelling was what I wanted to do, so I decided to leave Tarifa and thought about Portugal.

I had no more of a plan than follow the coast road to the north of Spain, taking whatever came my way.

After I said goodbye to friends, I took a detour through Seville, spent a night exploring the lively city, overnighted in Huelva and crossed the border into Portugal the next day.

From here, I drove one hundred kilometres west through Faro and toward Lagos, famous for its beaches and kitesurfing.

That night, I slept near Quarteira and carried on towards the old city the next morning.

It was here my plans went wrong.

As I drove towards Lagos, I hadn't realised but my sat nav had locked itself onto the centre of the old city. As I got close, I guessed what was happening, but drove on anyway straight into the old quarter.

It had not been designed with campervans in mind and, with a sickening crunch of metal on stone, I wedged my campervan between two buildings!

"Shit," I said out loud. I'd got stuck fast.

As I sat wondering what to do, a man appeared from one of the buildings I'd jammed into. He looked at my campervan, at me, at the walls, and shook his head. It was a surreal moment. I couldn't help but think *I should have stayed in Tarifa*.

"Don't move," he told me as he continued to shake his head, "or you'll have down my shop." But he then laughed and reassured me he would get me free.

I wasn't so sure. Neither were the queues of people building up behind me. But, all credit to him, he spent the next hour guiding me free while ignoring heckling crowds around us. Without his help, I don't know what I'd have done.

- - - - - - - - - - - -

After the traumatic introduction to life in Portugal, I explored the area of Lagos and stayed at the best kitesurfing spot I'd seen for a while. The river Alvor.

It didn't take long to settle into the green, warm, and windy part of the Algarvé. It was perfect for fitness training and kitesurfing, and other than writing my blog, for the next week I did little except experiment with food changes based on eating with a low glycemic index.

Until now, I'd never committed to anything like this. But, motivated by my detox, I was keen. And the rules were simple – eat separate carbohydrates and proteins, leave set gaps between meals, and avoid anything that raised blood sugar levels.

Just like Tarifa, the results were incredible. My energy levels increased, I lost body fat, and gained muscle mass. But what was also noticeable was that I was now living with contentment in what I was doing. Combining the training, healthy living, kitesurfing, and travel had done me a lot of good. But I suspected something else might be having an impact.

I'd begun a routine of meditation each morning straight after a run, ride, or swim. Even though this was only ten minutes, the practice was giving me headspace, and this also seemed to be having a great effect.

~ This is van life ~

The next two weeks passed quickly.

I left the Algarvé behind and followed the coast road through Sagres. From here, I continued to the most southwest point of mainland Europe before driving north towards Carrapateira where I kitesurfed by day and listened to DJs play house music on the beach by night.

As I drove another thirty kilometres north, I stopped in a small town called Aljezur to post a present back to the UK for a friend. I didn't see the taxi rank sign when I parked, and returned, after my errand, to a wheel clamp and a €150 release fee!

Continuing north still, I spent nights having cliff-top guitar jamming sessions with a Spanish couple I met in the small fishing village of Porto Covo, free-camped on cliff tops, and fell asleep to the sounds of waves rolling into tiny beach coves.

My next stop, two hundred kilometres north, found me kitesurfing the famous yet wild beach of Guincho. Here a rogue wave caught me off guard, picked me up, and dropped me on the beach – right in the path of a local photographer who took great pleasure in capturing the moment.

Whilst in the area, I also explored the city of Cascais and attended a bull running festival at a town called Alcochete with a local kitesurfer I'd met on a beach. The festival culminated with an all-night street party and dinner at a very hospitable family home of an Azulejo artist who, not only fed me, but gave fresh ideas on where to visit next – Lisbon and the neighbouring town of Belém.

Having spent so much time on the beach, I appreciated an idea to do something different. I treated myself to my first conventional campsite in six weeks, parked my campervan, and slept near the city.

~ A soulful mood in Belém and Lisbon ~

The following morning, I rode my pushbike along a cycle track and stopped first at the historic town of Belém – the city from which many Portuguese explorers set off from on their voyages of discovery.

I soon tired of wandering the old streets, found a restaurant and met, sitting at the bar, Marie-Neige.

We got on straight away and, after agreeing to spend the morning together, shared food, explored the local gardens and museums, and sampled the famous Pasteis de Nata.

I appreciated the company, but as she explained she was taking a few days for herself, after finding out one of her daughters had been diagnosed with a critical illness, I was stopped in my tracks.

This was a sad story. Her daughter did not have long to live. But as she explained about her own life, I listened in amazement. Rather than dwelling on how bad the situation was, she continued:

"I have, and continue to create, as many nice memories for my daughter and family while I can, because what other choice do I have."

All this put my life into perspective. My biggest worry seemed to be where to park my campervan for the night, or how to fit my training in-between travelling, and all that paled into insignificance when I thought about it.

- - - - - - - - - - - -

Once Marie-Neige left to return to France later that day, I collected my pushbike and, happy to have met her, continued to ride into Lisbon. My mind was thinking about my morning as I made my way straight to the older Alfama district. I really admired her way of thinking.

Within an hour of riding, I'd become lost in the labyrinth of steep streets and spent the afternoon dodging old-fashioned trams and took in the sights of the historic city with its mix of restaurants and homes, complete with washing hanging from tiny black window sills.

As the sun set, I cycled to the Bairro Alto district famous for the centre of the cities nightlife. This was a vibrant area full of people sitting drinking on steep steps that intersected busy streets, but again I hit a sense of loneliness. I shrugged the feeling off and continued to walk until I noticed a bar with crowds of people gathered outside.

As I got close, I heard an occasional burst of music followed by applause and, peering in through an open window, I looked into a dark, busy room where I saw a female singer and two men playing traditional Portuguese guitars.

I was in luck. In amongst all the different music on offer, I had found a bar playing Fado – the country's national music still surviving amid all the new street life.

I entered and took a spot at the bar, ordered a glass of wine, and became transfixed by the traditional, melancholy sounds. The words I didn't understand, but I sensed the mournful tune and lyrics. They had a sound of resignation, a sound of fate, and between the musicians and the singer, the audience, myself included, became captivated by the sounds.

The night finished at midnight and, as I collected my pushbike and rode back to my campervan, I knew my evening had ended well to an interesting and thoughtful kind of day.

~ Is it the mountain you conquer ~

After a few nights in the city, glad to have experienced something different from the beach, I turned east. I then drove three hundred kilometres to the Serra da Estrella mountain range.

This was the highest area in Continental Portugal. I was keen to explore the hills and climb the peak known as Torre, but I also wanted some quiet time and an opportunity to think about my next steps. The mountains seemed perfect for this.

That afternoon, I made the drive as far as Manteigasin and found an alpine-style village. It was more Swiss in look than Portuguese, with orange roofs and bright white buildings dotted in amongst dark green alpine trees. I found a street to park my campervan, walked the small town, and frequented a few bars to sample the local wines. The area seemed quiet, with a definite sense of a place not rushing to keep up with modern times and, that night, I slept well.

The next day, as I drove the winding roads and hairpin bends to the summit, I couldn't help but think I was cheating to access the summit of the mountain by road. As if to match my thoughts the weather turned bad and forbade me from seeing any of the views. But I didn't mind. Instead, I took it as a sign I should wait for the cloud to clear, parked my campervan, and spent the night on the top of the mountain.

The next morning, I woke to fine weather and could hike the open space of the mountains that had become visible. They were verdant, full of granite with odd shaped crags, gorges, and beautiful streams, interspersed with herds of roaming goats.

Because the hiking was good, I then decided to stay at the top of the mountain, settled into the quiet, and planned to give myself a training push for my triathlon.

For the next three days, as the sun rose, I rode my pushbike thirty kilometres down mountain roads, turned around, and in the hardest gear possible, rode back, then went for a run.

It was hard work, but as I did this every day, slept under the stars, and woke to incredible sunrises, I knew I was getting ready for my triathlon. But, as hoped, something else happened. The quiet time gave me the opportunity to realise I didn't want this adventure to become a quick break from work, nor slip back into an old way of living.

Instead, I wanted to create a set-up that worked for me. And there were things I could do. First, simplify my life back in the UK by giving up most of my material belongings and after that, step away from my remaining comfort – my house and home of thirteen years. This wasn't a new idea, but similar to leaving work I'd often questioned if I would make the break. But now I seemed to have built up momentum, and I wanted to use this to my advantage.

The next morning, with my intention clear, happy to have made the detour to the mountains, I left behind the highest point on mainland Portugal and continued to my next stop – the gritty city of Porto.

~ Sometimes it goes wrong at the end ~

On my way north, I stopped in a small town called Aveiro, known as the Venice of Portugal, and decided to sleep overnight.

I'm not sure why but once again I missed the company of others. To cheer myself up, I went out for dinner. Perhaps I looked forlorn, but as I queued for a table in a busy restaurant, a Portuguese family invited me to join them for food.

The parents spoke little English, but the daughter translated and it was a nice evening. This was just genuine hospitality. And, as they offered to give me a tour of their city the next day, and a look at how they lived, I recognised something warm and generous in the Portuguese. This was the third family I'd met in as many months who'd helped me, invited me for dinner, or who had just been fun to be with.

- - - - - - - - - - - -

The next morning, after a guided tour of the city and the realisation there was more to Aveiro than I'd first thought, I continued further north into Porto.

It was an hour's drive and, once arrived, I found a quiet area to park my campervan and explored.

I was intrigued to visit one of the oldest cities in Europe, known for its medieval riverside district and its Port and spent a few hours exploring the world's oldest bookstore, The Livraria Lello, before moving to the river Douro for a mandatory Port wine tasting tour.

It was fun, but a few days in the city proved enough for me and I was becoming conscious of time. I had been on the road almost four months and, even though life was good, I was thinking about my next steps and triathlon.

With that in mind, I re-joined the main route north, and continued up the coast to Esposende, hoping to find somewhere to kitesurf.

Thwarted by the lack of wind when I arrived, and to freshen up from the drive, I swam in a large flat warm water estuary. I thought it strange the water didn't taste salty and was full of large birds, but missed any implication of what this might mean.

That evening I planned where to drive next. I wanted to finish somewhere fun. I decided upon Viana do Castelo, and the next day continued farther north.

When I arrived, it looked great. A real 'jewel of the north' with a sandy beach, alpine forest backdrop, and an old style medieval city.

I parked my campervan in the forest and explored what I read to be Portugal's best kitesurfing. Straight away I saw the potential. There was flat water hidden behind a rocky outcrop perfect for practising tricks, and along the coast, solid looking waves pushed in by the Atlantic swell.

I was just thinking *I've saved the best until last, and I've still got a week to enjoy myself,* when I became ill. I couldn't believe it, I couldn't get ill now. I'd just booked a ferry to save the long drive through France and only had one week left in Portugal before I returned to the UK!

- - - - - - - - - - - -

At first, I ignored how sick I felt but as I began to spend more time on the toilet than anywhere else, I suspected something was seriously wrong.

By the third day, desperate to escape the confines of my campervan and hoping fresh air might do me some good, I dared to explore the streets of Viana do Castelo.

The change did me good. I felt better out in the open air, and that night, once I had returned to my campervan, I managed to eat, and for the first time in three days, I slept well.

In the morning, I felt better and went for an open ocean swim.

It started well but after fifteen minutes I became dizzy, got out of the water, and almost fainted as I got changed. I conceded then I needed help and made my way into the city.

I had seen Viana do Castelo had a lot of pharmacies so I chose one at random and explained my symptoms to a girl behind the counter. Within a few minutes of embarrassing questions and suppressed laughs, the staff told me I may have caught Salmonella from the warm water estuary I'd swam in.

I kicked myself. It was no wonder I had been ill. I was annoyed but there was nothing I could do now except take a course of probiotics and hope my suspected Salmonella would clear quickly.

~ Finishing strong ~

Two days later, I was on the mend, and able to venture out

without worrying about my illness. This had been the worse sickness I'd had for years, exaggerated by living in a campervan in a forest but at least I had a few days left to enjoy.

I got up early and rode up to a vantage point on which perched the Santa Luzia church. From here, I could look down over the Rio Lima estuary and see the curved sandy bay where I'd been sleeping. It was a perfect place to catch my thoughts. My return ferry date coincided with being on the road for four months. A third of the year had gone, just like that! But I felt good. I had made changes, lived on my own terms, and done what I'd wanted to do.

As I rode my pushbike back into town, I took my mind off the end of my adventure and found a nice restaurant. I took a seat, and happy to drink and eat again ordered a large glass of wine. After my recent illness and now size thirty waist, I figured I needed calories.

Then, out of the corner of my eye, I noticed two girls sitting with pushbikes loaded with luggage. It seemed polite to introduce myself and ask what they were doing.

They introduced themselves as Inés and Louise and told me they were on a political campaign through the country. They asked me to join them (for dinner, not the campaign), and quite liking the look of one of them, I agreed.

Both were nice girls. Conversations switched between what they were doing, and how I'd found Portugal as a traveller, until Inés explained she was the leader of the party she was promoting. This wasn't my usual topic of conversation, but I asked Louise what her role was.

She smiled and said: "Oh me, I'm the support crew, I fix the bikes and carry things, you see, we're a couple."

I left it there, but it was just my luck. She was very attractive.

- - - - - - - - - - - -

The next morning was my last in Portugal and I made my way to the beach early. I was keen to kitesurf one last time before

I tackled the long drive north to the coast of Spain and to the ferry terminal.

When I arrived at the beach, I found the wind was already blowing. I set-up my equipment, launched my kite, rode into the water, and played hard.

It was a good session. I crashed lots but landed a few new tricks I had been practising. I'd not improved as much as I'd hoped, but I now realised how good kitesurfing had been to have as a theme throughout this adventure. Not only because the sport connected me with people, but it had proven perfect to balance other adventures on the road.

Then, even though I could have stayed longer, I accepted my time in Portugal was at an end. I said goodbye to Viana do Castelo and a few people I had met and began my drive north through Spain. After four months on the road, to be leaving continental Europe didn't seem real.

After a few hours of driving, I crossed the border into Spain and followed the mountain road that took me through another part of the country I hadn't appreciated to be so beautiful, and began to accept I was on the way home. But, in the true spirit of adventure, the journey wasn't over yet.

I'd underestimated how far the drive to be and what I'd hoped to be a relaxing drive to take the ferry turned into a mad dash across the country. Not only did I lose my way on the mountain roads, almost run out of fuel, skipped a toll booth and narrowly escaped a fine, I came to within minutes of missing my expensive ferry home.

~ A chance to experience life ~

Once I'd parked my campervan on the ferry, checked into my cabin, and relaxed after the rushed drive, I realised I was buzzing!

I'd been on the road four months, visited three countries, driven 6000 miles, had a lot of new experiences, and met some incredible people.

As I remembered that first day on the road, I realised 'The

Curious Russian Fox' had been right – this hadn't been a holiday, this had been much more. And, as the boat moved from the Bay of Biscay and toward the Atlantic Ocean, my mind drifted back across my adventure.

I recognised now, before I'd left my job, I'd been ready to make a change and try something new. And today, having lived my dream, it was like I was a different person. Happy, content, and relaxed. Of course, I wasn't a different person, but something had shifted for me, and I wondered what had happened.

As I cast my mind back six months, I knew nothing had been wrong but when I'd set myself on a path of wanting to experience life, making a change was an obvious move.

But it hadn't been easy. Not only leaving work, but adjusting to my new-found-freedom. But both had taught me a lesson: if you change something externally, it doesn't always impact how you think and how you feel. As a cliché, I realised 'it comes from within.'

I decided then to walk the deck of the ferry and figure out how I'd adjusted into my new life. And, as I walked, it made sense.

The new experiences had done something akin to resetting me and, when I'd focused on things I'd valued – like my health, the travel, time with good people, and been in an environment which worked for me, my adventure had come together.

But there was something else which stood out. How things had come together when they'd seemed so unlikely. Like the opportunity to take voluntary redundancy; and all the people I'd met who provided me with what I'd needed, when I'd needed it.

Of course, it was my choice to recognise them for what they were at the time – opportunities to follow or ignore. But I couldn't help but wonder if I was being encouraged to stick to the path I'd chosen, because giving myself a chance to experience a different way of life had been exactly the right thing to have done.

Chapter 3
Getting Minimal

September 2015

> *Little is necessary for living a happy life.*
> *Marcus Aurelius - the last of the five good emperors of Rome*

~ Seeing an old world with new eyes ~

I'd been in the UK for a few days and, even though the novelty of running water, a fridge full of food, and a hot shower was luxury, coming home had proven a real shock. In fact, coming home had hit me like a tonne of bricks!

I was just thinking *a chat with a mate would help* when my phone rang. I smiled when I saw who was calling. It was Danny, a mate and avid supporter of my recent changes. I answered the call.

"Hi Danny."

"How's it going mate?" he replied.

"Great, but strange being home."

"I bet. So, come on, how are you getting on with being back in Derby?"

That was a fair question because I wasn't getting on with being back. In fact, I was struggling to understand how everything here seemed to be the same. This wasn't completely unexpected. I wasn't naïve enough to expect to drop into life here without a period of adjustment. But this was unreal.

As I explained this to Danny, he laughed and asked if I expected life here to be any different.

"I'm not sure," I told him. "But what came to mind when I returned is that I've driven back from a weekend kitesurfing in North Wales. In fact, for the first few nights, I was so unsettled I slept in my campervan instead of my house."

I heard him laugh. "You're going crazy," he said, "but I knew you would say that, especially on coming home from Wales. Nothing has changed here. Anyway, enough of this talk, let's meet for a beer. I'm curious what your plans are. Something tells me this isn't over for you yet."

We set a time to meet, ended the call, and I resigned myself to being home.

Of course, nothing had changed here. That's the way it goes. But because of my own changes, first with leaving work, then adjusting to travelling, and spending four months living in a campervan, to surround myself with my old life again was like I'd taken two steps forward and one step back!

But, as I reminded myself, this had been a choice. I snapped out of my mindset. I needed to get on with why I'd come back. Because Danny was right. This wasn't over for me yet. But I wondered if there was something else bothering me. And I think it was comfort.

If I stayed here I didn't have to think, plan, or move. There was nothing wrong with that, but I suspected I could easily find a job in an office, and be right back where I started. And, to be honest, it was quite a strong draw. But there was a saving grace.

For the past six months, I hadn't stayed in comfort and it had worked wonders. So, this told me to stick with the path to try and create something fresh, rather than go back to what I knew.

With that in mind, I reminded myself of my intention and gave myself six weeks to minimise my material possessions and made plans to move out of my house.

~ Goals, parallels, and motivations ~

It was September and two weeks had passed.

In that time, I'd made a start with my minimisation project, caught up with friends, and, perhaps as a way of coping with being surrounded by everything I knew, slipped into eating unhealthy food and drinking alcohol again!

But now, and ready for a break from sorting through my material life and focused on my next challenge, I drove one hundred and twenty miles east to the north Norfolk coast. It was time for my first triathlon.

This was an event I'd always wanted to do, and the idea pushed me out of my comfort zone. But I used this to my advantage.

Having not wanted to fail, I'd thrown myself into the training and returned from Europe fitter, leaner, and healthier than ever. Not bad for thirty-seven! But I also recognised parallels to other changes in my life.

Like going travelling, preparing for a triathlon had bought its own challenges but also its own benefits. Even though training had been a pain while moving, it had helped me settle into my new life. Both with travelling and returning home.

- - - - - - - - - - -

Once I had parked my campervan and got my bearings on the race, I made my way to the triathlon start area, placed my mountain bike in amongst the expensive road bikes, and got ready for the race.

I felt nervous, but I didn't mind. People seemed friendly, the weather perfect, and a small crowd formed to cheer us on, my family included, and I was glad for the support.

As I stood and prepared myself, a voice from behind me spoke:

"What the hell are those?"

I turned to see a competitor pointing to the pale orange oval-shaped balls, wrapped in cling film, hanging from my mountain bike frame.

"Homemade energy balls," I said. "I'm trying to avoid taking sugar gels. Do you want to try one?"

"Great idea," he replied, laughing, "but no thanks. They look like sheep testicles!"

I glanced to the balls. He was right.

An announcement then sounded over a tinny tannoy. It was time. All the contestants moved to the start line, put on bright orange swim caps, jumped in the water, and got ready to go. They looked like lemmings with bright orange heads dropping off a wall.

I had a moment of trepidation as I peered into the murky water of the harbour. It looked nothing like the azure sea of the South Coast of Portugal I'd trained in, but I jumped in, my head went under the water, and the cold engulfed me. But there was no time to think. I heard a loud bang, and the race began.

The 'professional' athletes swam hard and were soon in front. The rest of us scrambled, scraped, and pulled through the water until we settled into some kind of order.

I swam hard to get off to a strong start but when I looked up to check my position, I realised I had gone in the wrong direction. So much so, a man in a safety canoe paddled over to check I was OK. Embarrassed, I got into my stroke, completed the swim with no other dramas, and made it back to shore having caught up with a few stragglers.

As I peeled off my wetsuit, I stole a glance around to scope my position. At least I wasn't in last place. I spotted my niece and nephew cheering me on, jumped onto my bike, and rode off into the countryside.

I soon realised my disadvantage. My mountain bike was slow compared to the race bikes everyone else rode, and all those which had been behind me on the swim soon overtook me. By the time I'd completed the ride, dropped my mountain bike off, and got ready for the run, I was placed near the back. But I wasn't fazed. This is where the training counted.

A triathlete friend, Lisa, had told me to train for the transition between the bike and the run. I did and it hurt. But now I realised the effort had been worth it as my body adjusted, and I set my sights on those that had overtaken me on the bike stage.

"You're looking strong," shouted a spectator as I sprinted away from the bikes and got into my stride.

It was what I needed to hear.

The run was tough, but I pushed hard and picked people off as we cut through a forest, across a beach, and looped back round to the finishing straight until, forty-five minutes later, I crossed the finish line with my arms in the air. The race was done.

As I caught my breath and kept moving, I looked around for my family. I didn't see them at first.

"Your number?" asked a girl who stood handing out medals.

I told her, she moved to check a computer, then gave me my medal, time, and position. Three hours, seven minutes, and two hundred and twentieth out of two hundred and sixty. I would have jumped for joy if my legs had worked. I'd finished an hour quicker than hoped, and I wasn't last!

Then, I heard my sisters voice behind me.

"You're back," she said, looking confused.

"Yes, I'm back," I replied.

"Oh, we walked to the café for a drink. We missed you finishing. Sorry."

"What, so you got no photos of me crossing the finish line?"

"No, sorry. You were too quick. You told us you would be slower."

I laughed. It was typical. I had told them I would be slower, and they'd driven all the way to support me and missed the best bit. But I didn't mind. After all the effort of training, I was just pleased with what I'd achieved.

~ Getting minimal and moving on ~

After the triathlon, it was straight back to Derby to finish what I had started at home, and it didn't take long to realise I'd underestimated what I wanted to do.

My house required work before I could rent it. I owned a second 1977 Volkswagen campervan I'd loved and used for thirteen years which needed restoring. I just had so-much-stuff collected, and there was no magic formula to getting things done.

I even looked into paid storage until I realised the irony of paying someone to store my belongings so I could be more minimal!

But, by the end of November, after two months of sweat and tears, I knew I was getting close to achieving my minimalistic goal. Then, over the space of a week, and quite suddenly, I found a tenant for my house, sold my classic campervan, and moved back in with my parents – thirteen years after moving out!

It was good to move again, but it was also strange. Not only had I stepped away from my house and home, I'd left myself with little more than a few books, kitesurfing kites, a laptop, an old motorbike, and my other campervan. Not the norm for a thirty-seven-year-old. But there was more to it than that.

Over the years, I'd noticed having physical clutter tantamount to visual noise. Having realised the contrast by being away from it, I now understood it can be tiring when it surrounds you. So, what I hoped to create by getting rid of everything I didn't need was space, and a clear mind.

But now my priority was to decide upon the next adventure. I gave it some thought and decided on more travel. But this time a new experience. Something which included backpacking, volunteering work, and for good measure, some kitesurfing.

I looked at options and narrowed my decision down to two choices. Cape Town in South Africa, or the North-East coast of Mexico. I chose Cape Town, booked a return flight, and at once questioned my choice. I'm not sure why. Perhaps because this wasn't my first visit to Cape Town.

This continued for a few days until I shifted my thinking. Because there was more to South Africa than the Mother City.

This was a country that was both underrated for travel and fantastic value for money, with an opportunity to overland, volunteer, and kitesurf. Then I also discovered a vibrant yoga scene ran across the country.

Yoga had been something I'd started before I disappeared travelling around Europe and Morocco. Not only as a physical practice but as an aid to settling thoughts. I'd stumbled across it by chance after a relationship break-up, and it seemed to be a great technique.

In-between all the travelling and training for my triathlon, I'd let my practice slip whilst on the road. Having picked things back up with a new teacher in Derby, I'd been reminded how helpful it could be.

At a recent class, I'd mentioned my travel plans to my teacher and he'd encouraged me to keep practicing while travelling. It made sense. It could be a great way to meet new people and see another aspect of the country. So I did my research, found a studio close to where I planned to stay in Cape Town, and contacted a lady called Yvonne. It was now a valid option when I arrived.

Then, I got ready to leave. The idea was to spend Christmas at home with my family, fly on boxing day, land in Cape Town, see friends, kitesurf, and go from there.

I had no more of a plan than that and, to be honest, I didn't want one.

Chapter 4
New Experiences in South Africa

January 2016

Travel is the one thing that will make you richer.
DH Lawrence - novelist, poet, and playwright

~ Working with less control and more trust ~

Christmas passed and I said goodbye to friends and family.

"When will you be back," asked my dad, as he dropped me off at the National Express bus depot. I reminded him of my return flight in six weeks. He didn't seem to think I would be on it. And, if I was honest, neither did I.

Not that I had a definitive plan. I intended to stay in Cape Town for ten days, enjoy the lifestyle and kitesurfing, and travel across the country. I was working with less control, more trust, and I wondered how it would work out.

I took the soul-destroying National Express bus from Derby to London and flew the cheap seats via Dubai to the Mother City. Twenty-four hours later I came in over the famous Table Mountain, that, from the air, looked like a giant natural amphitheatre surrounding the city.

To the south of the mountain, I saw the Cape Peninsula, a scenic spine which jutted down into the Atlantic Ocean. To the east, the Cape Flats. And, to the north, the newer development. This is where I would stay. This is where the kitesurfing happened.

As I got into life on the Cape, I caught up with friends, celebrated New Year, and switched into travel modus. This time round I didn't need to adjust, it was straight into thinking about what to do next.

I explored options for volunteering at game reserves, but nothing seemed suitable. Even though I knew an established backpacking route to follow, I was looking for something different. But I didn't know what.

Instead, hoping to get clarity, I followed the yoga lead from the UK, found the studio, and the teacher Yvonne welcomed me into the class.

It was a strong practice. Much harder than what I'd done before, but once I got my head around the chanting, I loved it. Not only for the yoga. I also met some nice people who gave me ideas of things to do across the country, and a workable choice for my next move.

Yvonne had told me about a rehabilitation centre for big cats called Panthera Africa. They took volunteers and were based only two hour's drive from the city. The idea sounded great. I researched, liked what I read and, by email, asked to join them. They replied straight away. They were full. But I tried again and explained more about my own changes.

Two days later, I had my answer. I'm not sure what changed their minds, but the reply said yes and they asked me to join them in a few days. It seemed like my plan of less control, more trust, worked fine.

A few days later, I bid goodbye to friends in the city and made my way to the airport to be collected by the team at the sanctuary. And, as I did, I remembered what my dad had said about my return flight. He was right. There was no way I would be taking it now.

~ Panthera Africa - living with purpose ~

After following the road through the Hottentots-Holland mountain range towards the southern end of the Western Cape, I arrived at Panthera Africa – a forty hectare farm which served as the home of Lizaene and Cat. The creators of one of only seven safe havens for rescued big cats in South Africa.

I had never worked with animals and looked forward to doing something so different. For someone who has spent his whole life living in the industrial Midlands of the UK, I knew this would be special.

That night, I fell asleep to the sounds of lions roaring!

The following morning, after meeting other volunteers, Danni, a long-term volunteer from Australia, offered me a tour of the facility. I accepted, and we left the house behind and walked the grounds.

They seemed simple. A mix of small trees, sand, and typical African fynbos scrub, and set away from the house were a series of large enclosures. Being made of thin wire mesh, they reminded me of a large school tennis court. Until that is, I noticed the lion.

He was a large male, pale ochre with a darker mane, stretched out lengthways on top of what looked like a corrugated air raid shelter. As we got close, he sensed us, rolled onto his back, yawned and bared his long teeth.

"That's Obi," said Danni, smiling at my now stunned face. "One of five lions we have here."

We continued to walk and Danni explained three of the Panthera family lived here. Lion, leopard, and tiger, as well as caracals and jackals. She also explained the animals came from a captive and mistreated background. From what I saw, ten, maybe twelve separate enclosures placed in a giant u-shape.

Curious, I asked when the animals would be released.

"Never," she said, looking sad. "They were all born in captivity and it wouldn't be right to release them into the wild. None of them will ever be free. This is the reason Cat and Liz have created this sanctuary. It will offer a safe place for them to live out their days."

"I didn't realise there was a need for sanctuaries," I said to her, confused.

"Few people are aware," she replied, "Liz and Cat are trying to increase awareness and educate people about conditions big cats face in captivity. They are using Panthera Africa as a platform to help spread the word."

This came as a shock. I thought breeding in captivity to be a positive thing for conservation. But as Danni explained the stories behind the animals, I understood a very different story. From what I discerned, it seemed like exploitation of animals for profit. I thanked her for the insight and tour, and we walked back to the house.

Now it was time for work.

I teamed up with Adam, a volunteer from the Czech Republic, and Joseph, a full-time worker from Malawi. They were both great guys, and together we built a new shelter for the animals.

Whilst I shared travel stories with Adam, I listened with interest to Joseph's life. He was an interesting character and I warmed to his infectious smile and laugh. I could tell he liked being here. Not even a recent mugging where someone stabbed him in the arm as he visited friends in Cape Town had dampened his spirits.

I also enjoyed working on the farm, and the next few days passed quickly as I helped with planting trees, repaired electric fences, and dissected a cow to feed to the animals. It was hard work, and there was always a lot to do. But it was well balanced by an opportunity to be close to the animals.

Even if it was unnerving with a grown lion watching you work.

- - - - - - - - - - - -

By the end of the week, I'd extended my stay at Panthera, and because I had more time, I had a chance to speak with Liz and Cat. I was curious what had started this journey for them. They were happy to share their story.

They told me they'd both started as volunteers at an organisation supporting big cats where they'd discovered the animals were being exploited, so they created their own company. Liz worked in the industry already, but Cat had been a commercial real estate broker in Norway who was on sabbatical. She quit her job, moved to South Africa, and together they created Panthera Africa!

I was impressed, but there was more to understand. Because the facility conducts no cub petting, no breeding, or no animal trading, it may be classed as a true sanctuary. Not only providing a safe home for the animals, but in a position to educate the public about conditions these animals can face in captivity.

I couldn't help but be inspired. Not only by the courage it took to act for these animals but that Cat left a secure and high paid job in the city to follow what she believed in.

Then, I discovered they'd only been open nine months. They had done so much in a short time it proved to me what is possible with focus and commitment to something you believe in. And their passion showed because the whole place had a great energy. You could really feel it.

~ There's a deeper meaning (and a donkeys head) in the air ~

At the start of the second week, Cat asked who wanted to help feed the lions. I volunteered and then learnt a Norwegian TV crew were on site to do filming, and this would be part of a show.

I asked more and found out that Cat's cousin worked as a TV presenter in Norway. He had been living on the streets to help raise awareness of the homeless. He had met a recovering drug addict who'd wanted to visit South Africa, and now it was happening for him, here at Panthera Africa.

"Don't worry about it," she told me. "But will you clear the fence? Last time we missed, and it made a real mess."

With that in mind, but not sure what was meant, I wandered to the enclosures, met Joseph, and spotted the farm bakkie with a sheet draped over the rear. Flies buzzed everywhere, I guessed this to be the food, and pulling off the cover I faced a severed donkey head, a stack of large ribs, and chunks of what used to be hindquarters.

It was like a butchers truck.

Cat then wandered over, mentioned the head was for Obi, the lion, and we needed to start with that. I glanced around and noticed the film crew in close succession. I couldn't believe this was my life right now.

"Ready, John?" shouted Cat.

"Ready," I shouted back, failing to sound convincing, and grabbing the ears of the donkeys head, I lifted it off the truck. The head felt warm, its fur thick and bristly, and as I got an idea of its weight in my hands, blood dripped over my trainers. And these were my new and expensive trainers.

The head was heavier than I expected it to be, but it was too late now, I was committed, and I looked up at the fence I hoped to clear.

On the other side paced Obi – the five-year-old male lion, and, in the moment, I couldn't help wonder if this head represented my past life. Not that I'd ever decapitated anyone, but what better way to move on from something than by feeding it to a lion!

In the distance, I heard a countdown of "three, two, one, go," and I swung the head back, and launched it through the air.

At first, for a donkey's head, it flew well. But, as it clipped the top of the enclosure, I wasn't sure it would make it or fall back at my feet. But it cleared, the lion pounced, gripped the skull between his jaws, and dragged it off into the long grass.

"Did you get that?" I turned and asked the film crew stood beside me.

"We got it," they replied and gave me a thumbs up and a smile.

I gave them a big grin in return. Because today was Monday and, as my mind drifted back to the office job I'd left nine months ago, I knew my life could not have been any different.

Which was what I had wanted, and perhaps needed, from the start.

- - - - - - - - - - - -

Later that week, Liz asked if I had spent time near the animals. I hadn't, so that evening, as they became more active as the heat subsided, I visited the enclosures to sit with them.

They all seemed incredible but two had captured my attention. The first was Arabella, a young female tiger, and the other Achilles, an older male lion. I went to sit with the tiger first and waited until she became interested enough to investigate who stood in her territory.

Separated only by a thin wire fence, she came close, and I could take in her physical strength and striking colours. I knew I would be safe behind the fence but an instinct of fear ran through me. These were strong dangerous animals. But as she moved through the grass of her enclosure and lay down to within a metre of me, then lapped water which had collected, I noticed something else. She looked, unless I was mistaken, at peace.

When I moved to sit with Achilles, the lion, it was the same, and I couldn't help but be in awe of where I was. Their presence, together with the fading heat of the day and the sounds of the African bush, was quite a strong experience. But I was also sad. This wasn't their true natural habitat and, because of the impact of people, these majestic creatures had been confined to a sanctuary to protect them.

By the time I'd returned to the house, dark had set in and I bumped into Cat as she was leaving the grounds. She asked how my day had been. I smiled and told her great, but asked her something.

"This may sound a little crazy," I said to her, "but is this a rehabilitation centre for animals or people?"

She considered what I had said, laughed, and then replied.

"I think you get back what you put in, or perhaps what you need, but you're not the first person to ask, so I do wonder sometimes." Then, with an almost knowing glint in her eye, she smiled, bid me "goodnight," and left me with my thoughts.

Whatever was happening here worked. I had only been volunteering for two weeks but recognised what an incredible setting it had been to spend time in.

If that came from humans, animals, the environment, or good intentions, I guess I will never know. But my short visit had taught me one thing. Doing something with a deeper meaning makes for a much better experience, even when it takes more effort.

~ An open road and an open mind ~

After two weeks, it was time to leave Panthera Africa and start my road trip across the country.

I hired a car and gave myself two weeks to follow the five hundred kilometre stretch of road known as the Garden Route linking the Western and Eastern Cape. There, I planned to drop the car off. Then, in the name of doing something different, I hoped to find a boat and continue my journey along the coast towards Durban. I had two months until my visa expired.

I said goodbye to my new friends and, amazed at my first travel experience in South Africa, left the sanctuary, collected my brand new white Hyundai saloon, and began my drive.

- - - - - - - - - - - -

Over the next two weeks I enjoyed the Garden Route with its diverse vegetation, cliff top walks, and secluded rock pools which proved perfect for naked swims.

I explored the indigenous forests, kayaked the Storms River mouth, and shared a hike along the world famous Tsitsikamma trial with a friend, Helen, who I had met a few weeks ago in Cape Town on my first ever Tinder date. She was passing through on a business trip and, because experiences are better shared, we met and hung out for a few days.

Then, my plan changed.

As I arrived at the end of the Garden Route, marked by the industrial town of Port Elizabeth, I discovered the only way to continue my journey by boat was a cruise ship priced at €150 per night!

But I didn't worry. Instead, I extended my car hire, and remembered an idea from a friend Sally, who I had met at the yoga studio in Cape Town. She had suggested an eco-House called Terra Khaya located deep within the Amothole mountains.

I checked the map, decided to go for it, and drove three hundred kilometres to the centre of the Eastern Cape province and stopped at a village called Hogsback where the house was situated.

When I arrived, I was skeptical of a backpacker accommodation claiming to be eco-friendly. I didn't know if this would be my style of place. But I trusted the recommendation, reminded myself I was here for new experiences, and left preconceptions at the door.

From the outside it looked like a nice place. Like a giant Hansel and Gretel cottage. Once I had found the reception desk, I asked if I could stay a few nights. The man behind the counter with dreadlocks gave a quizzical expression, smiled, and said: "Yep that's what they all say."

He turned out to be right.

- - - - - - - - - - - -

Terra Khaya wasn't your average backpackers accommodation. This was a place for happy wanderers, adventurers, and the open-minded. It was simple, unconventional, and an eye opening experience.

Built using natural techniques and recycled materials, the main lodge and accommodation was a balance of rustic living with no compromise of style. Because it was at the top of a mountain, it was off the beaten track, and 100% off the grid. Limited electricity was provided by solar panels, hot water came from burning wattle – an alien invasive tree species, and the toilets were self-composting.

I soon learnt the name was both Latin and Xhosa and translated to Earth-Home. It promoted conscious living using permaculture principles, and similar to Panthera Africa, it showed what is possible with passion and commitment to what someone believed is worthwhile.

Over the next few days, as I settled into the house, I realised my visit had coincided with the start of a permaculture design course. People from all over the country had come to learn about healthy relationships with the land, and how to design landscapes mimicking nature while giving food and materials.

Until now, I had never heard of permaculture, but I was keen to immerse myself with the group to absorb by osmosis what I could. And it was a fun time. I soon learnt this was living which worked with, rather than against, the environment, and this really appealed.

Within the group there was also a sense of community and skill sharing, and it was after an evening of red wine and a conversation with the owner and creator, Shane, that I mentioned I was interested in yoga and set myself up for a challenge.

"You practice do you?" he said. "Great. How do you feel like leading a class tomorrow?"

"Sure," I replied. "Where can we do it?" I think it was the wine talking.

"On the grass outside. I've got mats for everybody. The whole group can join."

"Everybody?"

"Yep."

That night, I didn't get much sleep. Not only because of a wild storm that rolled in across the mountains but there were at least 30 people staying here.

But, despite my fears, it went well. I enjoyed leading it, everyone seemed appreciative, and I even got a free night's accommodation.

----- ----- -- -

Over the next week, I also spent time away from the house. It was a beautiful area and I hiked nearby forests, searched for waterfalls and natural pools, and breathed in the cool, damp, mountain air.

It was very relaxed and peaceful, and my quiet was only broken one day by a naked rambler who, I assumed because of his lack of clothes, had not expected to see anyone else that day! I'm sure he was staying at Terra Khaya, but when I looked for him that evening, he had already checked out.

Then, after ten days had passed, I decided to leave. There had been live musicians, huge fires, and a look at something I never thought I'd be interested in. I was surprised to find I had to pull myself away. But it wasn't just the house, it was the people.

I'd had great conversations, learnt something new, and had a fun time shared. But to leave was a choice I had to make to see more of the country.

So, I said my goodbyes, hugged people I'd met, and left Terra Khaya behind knowing my visit here had been very much worth it. I just had to keep an open mind to appreciate it.

~ Curiosity and the church ~

Once I'd extended my car hire, I followed the road one hundred and fifty kilometres south. First through East London, then east along a coast road which led me deep into a part of the Eastern Cape called the Wild Coast.

Known as the Transkei, this was part of the former homeland. I was heading to a backpacker accommodation called Bulungula lodge at the heart of a traditional Xhosa community.

It was a tough drive. Not only a long way, but single track gravel roads, in the rain, with no civilisation. By the time I'd arrived I was exhausted and night had fallen. Even my host seemed surprised to see me, welcoming me with:

"Oh, I didn't expect you would make it tonight."

I'm not sure where else I would have gone. There was nothing else around but I checked in and fell straight to sleep. This time, my accommodation was a tent perched in a tree.

- - - - - - - - - - - -

I woke early the next morning to the sound of water dripping on canvas and to the smell of damp wood and rain. I unzipped my door and climbed down a rickety ladder to investigate. The lodge stood perched on top of a hill, was open to the ocean on one side, and surrounded by fields on the others.

As I walked the grounds, I noticed several traditional African rondavels, each painted pink or turquoise. It seemed rural and traditional. For a moment, I missed Terra Khaya, but I pushed the thought out of my mind.

At breakfast, I quizzed the manager for recommendations of ideas of things to do.

"Take a walk around," he suggested, "there are no fences, crime, or beggars. Please explore the village."

Thanking him, I finished my coffee and began to explore the nearby beach and fields.

It was quiet, but as I walked and came close to the homes, I heard a noise what sounded like singing followed by a drumbeat. The sound was coming from the rondavels and, being curious, I went to look.

As I got closer to the round building, I saw the door open and, peering in, saw a room full of women dressed in bright clothes. They were stood in two groups and a man in his seventies, along with a boy who looked roughly ten years old, separated them.

The singing had stopped when I got there but the man spoke. I didn't understand the words but what he said resonated with the crowd. And as each sentence met with a strong chorus of "amen," I realised I had stumbled across a church, mid-ceremony.

As soon as the preacher finished speaking, the boy started to beat what appeared to be an old leather pillow. He was holding it in one hand and hitting it with the other. It worked well as a drum and as he hit a steady rhythm that got faster, the women danced. And I mean danced. They moved together, stamped the floor with their feet, stretched their arms to the ceiling, shook their hands, and shook their heads. It was one of the most expressive things I'd ever seen.

As I stood watching, someone inside noticed me, waved me in with a smile, and pointed to a plastic chair near the back of the room. I entered, and the energy in the small, hot, dusty space hit me. I took my seat and saw the people, guided by the man and boy, go from a fever pitched frenzy, to calm again. The service lasted another thirty minutes as the cycle repeated, and I sat there, amazed at what I was witnessing.

Once finished, not wanting to overstay my welcome, I made to leave and thanked whoever I could as I worked my way out of the busy space. Then, a hand grasped my arm. I turned and faced a young woman and she told me to wait. For a few moments there was a commotion, but the woman explained she spoke English and asked me to say a few words to the congregation.

"You want me to speak?" I asked her, confused.

"Yes," she replied, "and I will translate for you."

Put on the spot, I agreed, and once the crowd formed outside and settled on the grass, I stood.

"Hello everyone," I said. My words were met with blank faces.

"I'm from the UK and travelling through your country." More blank faces.

"I'm pleased and humbled to be in your village, and thanks for letting me into your church." My translator conveyed the words, and I saw people smile and nod. Deciding to finish on a positive, I stopped there.

Nodding thanks to the woman for translating I made to leave, but felt another pull on my arm. This time it was the preacher. Without saying a word he smiled and led me to his house.

When we arrived, I was offered a seat, and then, for the next hour, sat with other men from the village drinking tea and sharing traditional mieliepap porridge. My translator had disappeared and no-one spoke each other's language but this didn't matter. Even if it was curious, I was happy to have seen the village this way.

Later that night, once I had returned to my accommodation, I spoke with the manager of the lodge about my day. He seemed impressed I had been to church but I wanted to know something else. I'd noticed the women dancing had been clasping photographs of children in their hands and I wanted to know the significance.

What he said shocked me to the reality of life here. They held pictures of children who had died, and over half the homes in the village had lost at least one child. Now I understood the importance of the church.

He then became positive and explained: "The area has richness in other ways such as the community, land, and projects which work toward solving the challenges of poverty, and still promote traditional African culture."

Thanking him, I said goodnight and returned to my tent. I needed a chance to process my day.

Whilst glad to have seen part of the country with history and culture, the reality of life here was so different from anything I knew. *But perhaps,* I reminded myself as I fell asleep that night, *that was a very legitimate reason to travel in the first place.*

~ Getting good tidings in the mountains ~

After a few more nights, I left. Although there was more to experience, I was looking forward to doing something simple and physical.

I said my goodbyes, extended my car hire once again, and drove towards the range of mountains which bordered Lesotho, the Eastern Cape, and the KwaZulu-Natal province. From here I was going to the Drakensberg, or as they are known in Zulu, uKhahlamba – the barrier of Spears.

I drove four hundred kilometres north through Mthatha, the birthplace of Nelson Mandela, to a small town called Underberg where I entered the Southern National Park. I soon found a backpacker accommodation, settled in and met Daniel, from Holland. He was the same age as me and we were both keen to share a hike.

Daniel seemed to know the area and, after some discussion on routes, we agreed to meet early the next morning.

- - - - - - - - - - - -

The next day, Daniel suggested we tackle a long route known as Balancing Rocks. This was a route which worked its way up a steep hillside, past large granite boulders, and up to a height of a thousand meters.

I was happy to follow his suggestion, and we were soon on the way.

As we walked, I saw the landscape was verdant with soft hills rather than dramatic peaks, and three hours later, when we stopped to take in the views, we could see most of the southern range of mountains. To the right of where we stood was a steep winding road which led to the neighbouring country of Lesotho. This was the Sani Pass.

It looked stunning, and I asked Daniel if he would like to hike it tomorrow.

"I've already done it," he told me. "But you should do it, it's hard, but worth it." I decided I would.

We then continued with our hike, made it to the highest point an hour later, and retraced our steps back down. Four hours later, we were back at base and the air had turned humid. Rain threatened, and as we shared a beer that night, a wild storm rolled in and lit the surrounding sky with purple forked lightning.

It was a dramatic ending to a good first day in the mountains.

- - - - - - - - - - - -

The next morning, Daniel moved on to another part of the mountains and I made my way up the Sani Pass and into the country of Lesotho. But, as I walked, something didn't feel right. I hadn't slept and seemed to struggle to adjust to where I was.

I shrugged the unease off, put it down to being too old for dorm rooms with squeaking bunk beds, and after a three hour hike, entered the Kingdom of Lesotho through a mountaintop passport office.

At a height of 2800 meters the landscape looked different to yesterday – flat, barren, and also very windy. I explored and met two Basotho's who gave me a ride on their pony and then drank a beer in the so-called 'highest pub in Africa' before retracing my steps down with a view of the mountains.

I noticed then the walking had done me good and I was feeling myself again. So much so, I decided to drive straight to the Central Drakensberg, and to the area which contained the highest and most dramatic peaks.

After following the roads in a north-east direction for two hundred kilometres, I entered the Central Drakensburg, checked into a lodge close to the popular walks, and bumped into Daniel again. I'd hoped he would be here. We seemed to be following a similar path but out of sync.

Both of us were keen to share another hike and agreed to meet up early the next day.

- - - - - - - - - - - -

When I woke, the weather looked miserable. It was wet, dark, and cold. After some deliberation, we still went for the hike but then spent four hours being teased by glimpses of dark, primordial looking peaks through the cloud.

Even though it wasn't the best hike it didn't matter. I was just happy to be in such a wild environment, and as we walked, I got to know Daniel better. He was a free-spirited guy and kept me entertained with stories of his travels. Even more so when he pulled out a giant yellow Poncho, slid it over his head, and muttered something about "a giant Dutch condom!"

Once we had returned to the lodge, I spoke with other hikers and, because the weather was forecast to stay wet, I picked up ideas of where else to go.

"Get into the Royal Natal Park," I was told. "Follow the river along the Tugela gorge to the base of the Amphitheatre. It will be dry and the hike is worth the efforts."

I had heard of the Amphitheatre and seen pictures of what is often the cover shot for hiking in South Africa books. It sounded good. Daniel had his own agenda. So I decided to go for it.

The next morning, I drove three hundred kilometres north to the start of the Tugela gorge walk. It was easy to find. I signed a mountain hut register and began a four-hour hike which followed a river through a forest and ended at the vertical face of the Amphitheatre.

When I arrived, I saw it was impressive – hundreds of meters high, and just like the front of a giant castle: dark and impassable. As I explored the area, I tried to find a waterfall I could hear but not see, then made my way across slippery rocks, fell, and landed in a deep pool full of icy water!

After an hour of exploring, I accepted I'd gone as far as I could and walked back to my starting point. As I did, I thought about what I wanted to do next. I knew it was possible to get to the top of the Amphitheatre but the hike involved a chain ladder climb up the side of a mountain.

By the time I'd got back to my car, I'd made my decision. I checked my sat nav and then drove one hundred and fifty kilometres north to a town called Kestell, right on the edge of the Royal Natal Park.

Once I had arrived at the town, I found a backpacker accommodation called Karma's and checked in.

This was my kind of place. Much more of a family style house and the owner, Vera, was famous across the country for the unique jam recipes she exported. After some food, she gave me advice on where to hike and suggested I make an early start the next morning.

- - - - - - - - - - - -

As suggested, I left at sunrise and drove to the start of the chain ladder walk. The starting point was an hour away and began from a dusty car park accessible only by a potholed road.

Once I'd arrived, I signed into a hut manned by cold looking rangers keeping warm by a stove. I checked directions, and was told to follow a track up the side of the mountain.

The hike began from a height of 2500 metres and the visibility was almost zero but, as I walked, I found the route was obvious. An hour later, I came to a set of steel chain ladders which ran up a vertical and exposed rock face. Then, I saw Daniel coming from the opposite direction!

We stopped and spoke. He had slept out on the mountain and gave me rough directions of the way to follow. I told him where I was staying and we agreed to meet in the evening. Daniel then carried on his way and I scrambled up the ladders to reach the top of a flat plateau.

The weather was still cloudy and as I neared the top of the one hundred meter climb, I came face to face with two Basothos who sat waiting. They startled me. They had been hidden by the mist.

"Hi," they said, "do you have any food?"

They were shepherds tending whatever animals would survive at this height of 3000 metres. I caught my breath and shared what I could. They didn't speak much English other than "food please."

I stopped to speak for a few minutes before continuing across the flat plateau that formed the top of the Amphitheatre and, an hour later, came to the edge of the Amphitheatre and to the top of the waterfall I'd heard yesterday.

This, I now realised, was the start of Tugela falls – the second highest waterfall in the world. It was mind-blowing being this high up.

Stretched out in front, I could see the Escarpment – a one thousand metre drop which stretched left and right for miles and, beyond that, there was nothing but open space and green mountain valleys. There was no safety rope, no barriers, and no warning signs.

I decided then to sit and soak in the scenery and, as I did, I thought back over my week. I'd walked a lot of distance and driven a lot of kilometres but this had given me chance to process my time in South Africa.

In two months, I'd experienced things I would never have dreamt of a year ago. Which is what I'd hoped for – some new experiences that would give me a shake-up. But I'd also got to a point where I'd needed to let everything sink in. And, with carefree walking being the one thing to focus on, I was glad to find it had worked.

~ The no plan plan delivers again ~

After so much time inland, and tempted by stories of coral reefs and tropical forests, I drove four hundred kilometres east toward the Indian Ocean. I was heading for the iSimangaliso Wetland Park, on the border of Mozambique.

I hoped to visit the Sodwana Bay National Park. This was as far from Cape Town as I could get whilst still being in South Africa.

The developed roads took me across the hot, humid KwaZulu-Natal province. Here I stopped to soak in the serene atmosphere of the battlefield sights of Rorke's Drift and Isandlwana. Then, I explored the areas which marked the first significant battles of the Anglo-Zulu War. There were many white cairns marking the fallen.

I spent the night in Dundee and, that evening, witnessed an incredible tropical storm. The rain that fell was amazing. Heavy, warm, and a lot of it.

The next day, I made it to iSimangaliso and entered the park itself where, in the space of an hour, I saw two endangered black rhino, a herd of water buffalo, and various kudu with their trademark spiral antlers.

Later that evening, after more driving, I arrived at my destination of Sodwana Bay.

The small village comprised of a few shops, a sandy road, and a strip of narrow forest covered dunes. I quickly found a place to sleep called Natural Moments. The accommodation was low key, rustic, and I soon settled in.

Then things got even better. As I spoke to the owner of my accommodation, Tracey, she asked if I was here to scuba dive.

"Actually I'm here to snorkel and explore," I told her. "Why do you ask?"

"Because this is one of the world's top scuba diving locations," she told me, laughing. "Didn't you know?"

I didn't know. I was just here to snorkel. But I soon found out this was an area which boasted a fifty-kilometre reef complex with hard and soft coral, and thousands of fish species.

I couldn't believe my luck and, keen to make the most of the opportunity, I signed up for a scuba dive course and got ready for a whole new underwater experience.

- - - - - - - - - - - -

The next day, I began my one-to-one scuba dive training.

My timing here coincided with the low season and, after a morning in a classroom and swimming pool, I was ready for my first ocean dive and we made our way to the beach to collect our diving equipment.

We set up and then launched an inflatable boat from the beach, cut a path through the ocean swell, and twenty minutes later stopped at a dive site known as Two Mile Reef.

As we prepared to enter the water, I had a quick reality check. Today was Monday, and I'd arrived yesterday. I had started dive training and was about to enter a whole new world! As I heard the shout of "get ready," I focused on where I was. This was happening.

Rolling backwards off the side of the boat, we dropped into the water and sank down to the reef at a depth of ten metres. It was like entering a different world. Peaceful and surreal. As I adjusted to the water and remembered my training, I kept breathing slowly in and slowly out. Not holding my breath.

Then, I felt a strong tug on my hand. My instructor Hans signalled me to look, and I saw a shark, twenty metres away, gliding towards us. Then I saw another. I tensed as they came close to us. They were white tip reef sharks, each about a metre and a half long. They didn't seem bothered as they circled, keeping their bodies side on to us. Until, with a flick of their tails, they disappeared.

Hans gave me the all OK sign, and we continued to explore the colourful reef until, forty minutes later, low on air and out of time, we returned to the boat and drove back to base. All of us were full of excitement at what we'd seen.

After lunch and more training, I was ready for my second dive. We took the boat once again, but before we arrived at the site, we had the chance to snorkel with pods of dolphins. They came right up to our boat, flipping and spinning.

The boat driver stopped the engine, we geared up with masks and fins, and dropped in the water with them. The dolphins were as curious with us as we were with them, until, five minutes later, they were gone, and we continued with our dive.

- - - - - - - - - - - -

The next five days continued in a similar way, and by the end of the week I was qualified to dive to a depth of twelve metres.

Whilst the rest of the week had brought no more shark or dolphin sightings, it had given me an interesting look at another world full of ocean life. I had come face to face with a puffer fish, almost put my hand on a scorpion fish, saw a lot of sea slugs, and even added an acute bout of seasickness to my experience.

I heard the variety and amount of life here was, in part, due to sea pirates off the coast of Somalia driving away Far Eastern illegal fishing trawlers. I didn't know if that was true, but if it was, then perhaps not all pirates are bad. But, what I'd enjoyed most about my time, was a simple week of fun with a team passionate about their job.

Many were from South Africa working as dive instructors. Others were from different parts of Europe building up experience or conducting marine biology research. It was definitely a lifestyle choice, and I doubted much money was involved, but everyone was happy with what they were doing.

In fact, the whole area seemed paradise for anyone with an interest in the ocean. And, after speaking with Tracey, the owner of the accommodation I was staying, I learnt that Sodwana, in Zulu, translated to 'little paradise on its own,' I could understand why.

~ Why no expectations can be a good thing ~

After ten days, I decided to drive to Swaziland.

When I'd began this road trip a month ago, I'd not considered visiting the small landlocked monarchy. But, when I realised the country lay between here and my next planned destination, Kruger National Park, I opted to stop and look.

I said goodbye to my host Tracey, ate a quick meal of Bunny Chow (a hollowed out loaf of bread filled with curry) and left the wetlands behind.

It was an easy one hundred and fifty kilometre drive north-west to the border of Swaziland, but as I entered the country I was asked to show insurance for my car. I had no documents, but I offered the guard a random piece of paper.

This sufficed, and I entered the country with no trouble, and with no expectations.

- - - - - - - - - - -

Swaziland is renowned for its hiking trails, cultural centres, and wilderness reserves, so I based my detour on that and checked into a backpacker accommodation close to the Ezulwini Valley for two days.

From here, I hiked the twin peaks of the Malagwane Hill, known as Sheba's breasts (said to have inspired King Solomon's mines, the first English adventure novel set in Africa) before exploring a cultural centre which contained the countries famous entertainment venue – the House on Fire.

I then continued fifty kilometres up through the country. Tomorrow would be my birthday and I hoped to find somewhere nice to stay.

As I drove, I noticed Swazi-style beehive huts set back from the road. They looked like the rondavels I'd seen in the Transkei, but darker.

I stopped, found the reception, and enquired the price. It was five times my budget, and I asked for cheaper options.

With a raised eyebrow, the lady behind the counter took me to a converted horse stable away from the main complex.

"The stable is empty tonight," she said, as she showed me around. "So, if you want to stay here, then they are all yours."

I looked round and noticed at least thirty small rooms, each with four beds hidden behind stable doors. It wasn't what I'd expected, but it came with novelty value. So I agreed, paid, and went to bed.

- - - - - - - - - - -

It turned out to be a mistake.

Like a cross between a bad nativity play and a horror film, I was kept awake by creaking doors, banging windows, and mosquitoes, and the next day, when I got dressed for my thirty-eighth birthday, I felt terrible.

At breakfast, the manager sensed something was wrong and asked if I was OK. I explained my story, tried to look pissed off, and mentioned my birthday was today. He listened to what I said, and then offered to upgrade me for free, into the luxury beehives.

"But on one condition," he continued. "You must buy a birthday cake, and share it with the staff."

"No problem," I told him, "I'll go for a hike and then drive to the city to collect one." I don't think he believed I'd do it.

That afternoon, once I'd finished a short hike around a nature reserve, I drove to the closest city of Mbabane, parked my car, and looked towards a bustling complex of shops, restaurants, and people. I had absolutely no idea where to find a cake. Then, from out of nowhere, two young men approached me.

"We want your car," they said and smiled at me. I laughed, told them the car wasn't mine to give, and asked if they knew where I could buy a birthday cake.

"Sure," they said, and pointed at a shop on the corner of a busy street. "In there."

I was dubious but went to look, and emerged from the shop fifteen minutes later, half expecting to find my car stolen, with a cake embossed with 'Happy Birthday'.

I couldn't believe what had happened. In a city of 50,000 people, I'd parked at random, and then been helped by two strangers who'd come to speak. Did they really want my car, or was there something else conspiring in my favour here.

Either way I got my upgrade, and the staff enjoyed the cake.

- - - - - - - - - - - -

I then stayed three more nights at the resort.

It gave me a chance to catch up on sleep and learn how to ride a horse on the open Swazi plains with the help of a local horseman, Star. This was another enjoyable experience and not what I'd ever considered I would like.

Which summed up my whole time in Swaziland.

Not as exciting as learning to scuba dive with sharks, or as awe-inspiring as working with lions and tigers. Instead just different, relaxed, and easygoing. Most of the time.

~ Expectation has a habit to set you up ~

Before I left Swaziland, I had to ring the car rental office to extend my hire again. They were curious how I was living my life week by week, but agreed.

After saying goodbye to my hosts at the resort, I continued north, crossed the border back into South Africa, and continued towards the Kruger National Park.

I had read Kruger covered an area the size of Israel and is one of the largest parks set up in South Africa. It also forms part of the Great Limpopo Transfrontier Park, linking both Zimbabwe and Mozambique. Kruger is the flagship game reserve of the country and, perhaps unfairly, came with expectations.

After a few hours of driving, I entered by a southern gate and got my bearings. From here, I planned to drive up, find somewhere to sleep in the park, or exit by a gate on the west side and return tomorrow. It sounded easy. And it was. Which came with a downside.

Because the park was so geared up for tourists with such well-maintained infrastructure, every animal risked crowding by brand-new-four-wheel-drives. It wasn't a big problem, but it took away the wild element I'd hoped for. But, it was possible to lose the crowds if I left the sealed roads and followed the less used gravel tracks which cut through the park.

Here, I saw the animals in a more natural environment. First a herd of elephants that appeared from the undergrowth with ears flapping and trunks swinging. Because they tended a calf, they stood and faced me until I backed my car away. Then, as I kept exploring, kudu and water buffalo. Finally, towards the end of the day, a pack of zebra, and three giraffes which I saw stretch their necks up to the tops of trees and chew leaves as small birds perched on their noses.

Despite the less than wild element, I still enjoyed a good day. But I wondered if I entered the park at dawn, just as the gates opened, when the temperature was cooler and roads quieter, I would have a different experience.

It seemed like a failsafe plan and I exited through a gate on the west side of the park, found a backpacker accommodation to sleep, and made plans to return.

- - - - - - - - - - - -

The next morning at five, I drove through one of the poorest townships I had seen in the country and re-entered by another gate. But it took a while to enjoy what I was doing.

In the space of an hour, I had gone from a decent accommodation, through a very poor township, and then paid an expensive fee to enter a developed national park. Similar to what I had seen in the Transkei a few weeks ago, it was such a massive contrast of how people lived.

Then, as if to match my mood, I saw nothing for hours. So much for my failsafe plan!

It wasn't until lunchtime when rains came and the roads flooded that I caught sight of the only animal for the day – an African wild dog, orange and black, with yellow teeth and dark eyes. He was unfazed by me as I parked to watch him lap up water from puddles collected on the road.

I decided then I had seen enough. I was glad to have driven through, but it wasn't quite the authentic African safari experience I'd hoped for.

With that in mind, I left the park and began a four hundred kilometre drive south-west towards the city of Johannesburg.

This was the final part of my journey across a country that had captured my heart with its people, landscapes, and wild elements – a train ride of 1500 kilometres and twenty-six hours which would take me back to the Mother City.

But first, I needed to find somewhere to clean my car. It was filthy from the past few months of road tripping across parts of the country I shouldn't have been.

~ A pleasant journey back ~

After tipping the valets who restored my hire car to its former glory, I dropped it off at Johannesburg train station, and prepared for the next part of my travels. As I did, I realised someone had left a backpack in the boot.

It must have belonged to one of the volunteers from Terra Khaya. I couldn't get it to them now, so I gave the bag to the man working behind the counter at the car hire desk. His face lit up when he realised it was a gift.

I then walked to the concourse to collect my ticket. I had been warned trains in South Africa were dangerous but I had researched my choice. This route was not only safe, but an under-utilised and cheap way to travel.

The train soon arrived, decorated with the purple, yellow and blue branding of the Shoshaloza Meyl company. Which stood for, I hoped would be true, 'a pleasant journey.' I boarded, found my cabin, and met my travelling companion.

He was an older gentleman, dressed smart and reminded me of Morgan Freeman. I offered him my hand and introduced myself. He did the same, smiled, and told me he came from the Transkei but was visiting family in Cape Town. As I spoke to him I sensed a man of dignity and calm, and as the train departed and left Johannesburg behind, I knew I had been lucky with my roommate. These cabins could hold four people and I could have ended up with anyone.

As I settled into my cabin, I let the past few months wash over me. And, just like returning from Europe, I was amazed at what an adventure it had been.

From the city to the sanctuary, the Wild Coast to the mountains, the ocean to landlocked Swaziland. All the national parks, the animals, landscapes, and people. South Africa had been full of surprises, and sitting here now, I knew there was a lot more to this country than I'd first imagined.

While it hadn't been easy to make friends and then move on; or to have seen poverty; or spent many an hour parked in a petrol station trying to find somewhere to sleep, phone in one hand, guidebook in the other; I knew the time had been worth it. Not only for a fun time, but because of what I'd experienced.

I decided then to leave my cabin and explore the train. As I walked, I wondered if the past few months had taught me more than I realised. *Perhaps*, I thought, but rather than getting stuck on it, I just let my thoughts run as I wandered through the carriages.

There wasn't much to see, except a few drunken men in the restaurant carriage and that each carriage had a guard carrying a 9mm pistol.

Unsure if this was a good thing or not, I returned to my cabin to relax, then sat and watched scenery change from city to veld, and to the dry, arid Karoo. It wasn't that interesting, but I didn't mind. I was just happy to sit back and think over the past few months of travel and adventure.

~ Happy, content, and very much alive ~

By the morning of the following day, we'd entered the Cape Winelands and Table Mountain came into view.

We soon rolled into Cape Town railway station, my travel companion said goodbye, shook my hand, and wished me luck. As I followed him off the train and onto the platform and entered the streets, the pace of the city hit me.

For a moment, I wasn't sure I liked being back, but I pushed the doubt from my mind.

I had spent enough time solo travelling, and I was looking forward to seeing friends for my remaining time in the country.

- - - - - - - - - - - -

Over the next few days, as I settled back into the city life, people told me "I looked well," and "travelling seemed to suit me." It was a nice thing to hear and, now I was back and had the chance to appreciate my adventure, I suspected exposure to a life beyond what I knew had done me a lot of good.

Having wanted to backpack across this country, not only was I pleased at what I'd done, I was certain the new experiences had shaken me up, given a fresh outlook, and helped reinvigorate me from a busy period of minimising my life and moving out of my home.

Because, right now, I was feeling happy, content, and very much alive!

- - - - - - - - - - - -

My final few days in the city then passed quickly.

I volunteered at a dogs rescue centre helping to build shelters; lost my trainers during a moonlight swim; practised yoga; and managed a final kitesurfing session. But this was no ordinary session – this was a sunset supermoon session.

What started like any other strong wind surf on the water, with the setting sun behind Table Mountain and a rising moon above the coastline, developed into one of the best kitesurfing sessions I'd ever had. To be surrounded by kitesurfers attempting tricks twenty metres in the air, silhouetted against the sun or the moon, was an unforgettable experience!

But then, a day later, my visa expired, and it was time to leave this amazing country. I wondered what to do. I could extend my visa and stay, or travel to a new destination. But I decided to travel back to the UK.

I felt confident it would only be for a short time, and it would be a good way to take stock, see friends and family, and share my adventure with others before deciding what to do next.

So, feeling happy and contented with how things had unfolded, knowing an open mind had bought some incredible experiences, I said goodbye to Cape Town, and flew back to the UK.

A Look at My Adventures
Images from the Journey

The journey begins, UK

Kitesurfers in Tarifa, Spain

Sunset, Tarifa

Hiking to a traditional Berber village, High Atlas mountains, Morocco

Snake charmers, Jamaa el Fna square, Marrakesh

Camel safari, Merzouga

On the road from Ouarzazate to Merzouga

Guitar jamming, Porto Covo, Portugal

I'm the small one on the left. Vanlife,
Guincho beach, Portugal

Triathlon, Wells-next-the-Sea, North Norfolk Coast

Kitesurfers with a backdrop of Table Mountain, Cape Town

Kitesurfing at Langebaan, Western Cape, South Africa

The donkey's head at Panthera Africa, Western Cape

One of the lions at Panthera Africa

Hiking the Sani Pass, border of KwaZulu Natal, South
Africa and Mokhotlong, Lesotho

Rustic accommodation at Terra Khaya,
Hogsback, South Africa

Flat water lagoons can be perfect for kitesurfing! North Western Province, Sri Lanka

Uda Walawe National Park, Uva, Sri Lanka

Getting the bike fixed, Sri Lanka

Teaching yoga at the Cape Town Kite Club, Big Bay, Cape Town

An *In Memory* mural of Cape Town rapper Bonzaya,
Woodstock, Cape Town

Rhosneigr beach, North Wales

Campervan life, North Norfolk Coast

Chapter 5
A Quick Stop in the UK

April 2016

A little step may be the beginning of a great journey.
Unknown

~ The freedom of nothing ~

As I sat in the rear of the taxicab that drove me from the train station to my parents' house in the UK, I noticed the first signs of Spring. Flowers were showing, and the air felt mild. And it didn't seem too bad being back.

Not only had it been an excellent plan to escape the UK winter, I was, in a material sense at least, returning to the freedom of nothing. Yet, I still knew I was moving forward.

Of course, Derby was a long way from Cape Town, lions, eco-houses, and scuba diving. But I now understood the result of stepping away from my house and minimising most of my material life. Similar to when I'd returned from Europe, everything seemed the same – the streets, the people, the landscape. The real difference was in my mind.

Not only had I physically moved on from my house and my belongings, I had mentally done the same. As hoped, I'd created space for myself. Which meant I was free for whatever was next. Even if it was unsettling to have no job, or home, to call my own.

But I had something else. Something much more important. My freedom. That, and a cunning plan to help me adjust into the UK.

My family were on holiday in Wales and did not realise I'd returned. I spent two days at their house and then, because I knew where they would be, drove my campervan to track them down. They were right where I expected – on the beach having a barbecue with friends. I strolled over and said "hi."

It was brilliant. They were all taken aback and I achieved maximum shock value. Not only were they surprised to see me, they'd even missed me. I'm not sure who was more surprised, them, or me!

I then spent the week filling them in with recent adventures, had impromptu pub lock-ins and guitar jamming sessions with ladies of the village where we stayed, explored the Welsh countryside, and relaxed.

Even though the weather was cold, and I missed the lifestyle of South Africa, I enjoyed living in my campervan and reminded myself I'd come back to take stock.

So, when my family returned home a few days later, I stayed where I was, and made a start on how I would do that.

~ An idea for a new purpose ~

My friends said I was delaying the inevitable when I told them I would stay in Wales. They may have been right, but if that inevitable included returning to my old life, I was not only delaying it, I was avoiding it at all costs.

This wasn't in a denial way. It was more of a spending time in solitude whilst enjoying myself with no distractions way.

I wanted chance to process recent adventures, and I needed time to consider what to do next. So I grabbed the opportunity to explore my country on my own, and I would start where I was right now. The Welsh Pembrokeshire coast.

I wasn't disappointed. The UK has incredible places if you know where to look, and the weather was on my side. I hiked dramatic coastlines in blazing sunshine, kitesurfed empty windswept beaches, and visited friends in the area. Even though this wasn't as dynamic and exciting as South Africa, it proved a healthy way to ease back into UK life, and it also gave me a chance to think back over the year.

While returning to the UK had seemed easier this time around, and I knew the changes I had made towards minimising my life had been worth the effort, what about the travelling? It had been my focus for a year, but had I done enough.

The answer was yes. At least for now.

Even though I was tempted to book a flight to South America and explore Peru, or drive my campervan into Europe again, instead, I wanted a new project. So I decided to turn the blog I'd written when I'd started travelling into a book

The idea had been floating around in my mind since I'd seen my parents. But now, standing on a beach in the South-West corner of Wales, one I'd not been to in over thirty years, it made sense. Not only did I want to capture my adventure in full, I suspected it would be great for processing everything that had happened.

So, with that in mind, I made a start on the writing.

~ Taking a different approach ~

The writing started well and I found it easy to map a story of what I'd done and where I'd been. But, after a few weeks, I realised all I'd written about was quitting my job and going travelling. And I couldn't help wonder if there was more to it.

When I thought about it, I knew I'd not just gone travelling. Instead, I'd given up on a career with security and comfort and swapped it for a life of freedom and instability. Then, for good measure, I'd sold most of my things, moved back in with my parents, and sometimes lived in a campervan. Not exactly the conventional life!

But this got me thinking. I felt happier now than I had done for years. I was no expert, but perhaps I had started upon my own journey of change. I'm sure my lifestyle wouldn't suit everybody, and I'd taken a risk to make it happen and there was more to come, but why not include how I'd found my experiences so far.

With that in mind, I got back to work on my book. Little did I know of the effort that would be involved.

Chapter 6
Sri Lanka

June 2016

It is not enough to be busy; so are the ants. The question is: What are we busy about.
Henry David Thoreau - American poet, and philosopher

~ Slow travel, with a purpose ~

Three weeks in Wales passed and I returned to my parents' house.

The time kitesurfing, hiking, and exploring had helped me adjust into UK life and I'd made another attempt with my writing. But, I'd realised, sitting at my parents' home, that this project would not happen instantly. So I decided I wanted a change.

Because I had no obligation to stay in the UK and write, I looked where I could be based that would be warm, sunny, and windy. I discovered there was great kitesurfing on offer in Sri Lanka. Then, I read that two of the UK's most renowned kitesurfing coaches, Christian and Karine, would be there for the next month.

This got me thinking.

I'd always wanted to have kitesurfing coaching. My level of kitesurfing was OK, but I had stopped progressing. So what better way than having coaching in Asia, focusing on what I enjoyed, to help me progress whilst also giving me inspiration to write!

Christian and Karine's website read *no spaces available* on their coaching courses but I called them anyway.

After a quick conversation, they told me they could squeeze me in if I didn't mind sharing a room. Things were coming together. But then I procrastinated. The course was expensive; the flight price increased overnight; there was no guarantee it would inspire my writing, and I didn't think it would happen.

Then, I inherited a small sum of money from a family friend. It was enough to cover the coaching, and thinking I was being told I should go for it, I booked onto the following weeks training. I would leave in a week.

But then, the next day, at a family barbecue, I injured myself.

It was my fault. I was playing football with my niece and nephew without wearing shoes and hurt my toe. A visit to accident and emergency confirmed a fracture, and a doctor advised I needed at least six weeks for it to heal. But I didn't have six weeks. I had six days.

This reminded me of the problems with my campervan last year. Why did this have to happen now?

I explained my plans to the doctor and asked his advice.

"Your call," he told me. "By the sounds of what you tell me, kitesurfing will hurt. But you could strap up your toes, take strong painkillers, and get on with it."

"Are you serious?" I asked him.

"Yes," he told me. "Sounds like a great trip. It would be a shame to miss your chance."

This wasn't what I'd expected him to say, but I liked the advice because it meant I still had a plan. Now I could get excited again. If I based myself in Sri Lanka and focused on the kitesurfing plus the writing, this would be slow travel with a purpose.

~ It's good to be moving ~

Five days later, I said goodbye to friends and family and took the train to London.

The city seemed busier than usual. I battled with people and argued with a man in a toilet after I knocked him over with the bag which carried my kitesurfing equipment, but I eventually made it to Heathrow Airport, checked in, and caught my flight.

Low season meant the plane was almost empty and I had four seats to myself. I stretched back, fell asleep, and dreamt of tropical beaches, strong winds, and fun times to come.

Ten hours later I arrived into Sri Lanka feeling refreshed, and cleared the most bizarre duty-free I had ever seen (full of washing machines, TV's, and hoovers).

As I left the airport and stepped outside, I faced a world of noise, colour, and smell. In terms of a contrast to the UK, this was definitely different, and hopefully inspiring.

I soon found a taxi and began the three-hour drive up the west side of the country to the kitesurfing locations.

The roads were crazy! Everybody seemed to be in a hurry. Buses overtook buses, cars overtook the three wheeled tuk-tuks, and motorbikes wove in and out of everybody else.

Two hours later, once we'd reached the town of Puttalam in the North-West of the island, we branched off to continue through a more remote part of the country.

Life was much quieter here. The land comprised a thin peninsula which jutted out from the mainland. This formed lagoons exposed to the strong winds but protected from the ocean swell. This meant perfect conditions for freestyle kitesurfing.

An hour later, we arrived at the small fishing village of Kapaladi, and I checked in to my home for ten days - Kite Kuda.

This was one of the first dedicated kitesurf camps on the island. It looked simple, was surrounded by sand dunes, nestled under palm trees, and looked just like what I needed. I quickly settled in, and because I'd wanted to acclimatise myself before the coaching began, I'd arrived a few days ahead of the rest of the group, and went to explore the village by foot.

As I walked, I could see it was simple. There were no roads, only sandy tracks accessible by four-wheel drive, motorbike, or tuk-tuk. The houses were built from concrete blocks, wooden poles, and coconut tree leaves. There was an occasional shop selling biscuits and cigarettes, a small school, and children running through the streets.

Then I spotted the kitesurfing location – three flat water lagoons separated by tall grass banks, fringed by sand on one side, and coconut trees the other. There were other kitesurfers on the water so I walked back to my accommodation, collected my kitesurfing equipment, set up, and joined them.

It was a great session. The water was warm, and the wind strong. And as long as I stayed careful my fractured toe seemed manageable. With that peace of mind, I could now relax into being here.

~ Coaching is not just for professionals ~

Over the next few days, the rest of the group arrived.

There were ten of us in total. An international mix from Europe, Asia, and Australasia. Everyone seemed friendly, keen to progress their kitesurfing skills, and have fun at the same time. After introductions, a few drinks, and an early night, the coaching began.

I was excited for this. For now, at least, the writing would have to wait.

The routine for the week seemed simple. Get up early, eat a healthy Sri Lankan style breakfast, make our way to the beach, set aims with Christian and Karine, and get on the water and kitesurf.

The first day the wind blew hard. Everyone was full of excitement, set up their equipment, and went all out until tired bodies forced a rest. But we soon learnt there was no excuse for being slack or lazy. After a fresh coconut from a local vendor, and some coaching with Christian and Karine, it was back onto the water again for more trick attempts, crashes, and painful landings.

As the day progressed, I found the location perfect for training. The conditions were ideal with flat water; it was warm, and the lagoon was small. This encouraged you to try a trick in one direction and then turn round fast, otherwise you would literally end up in a coconut tree.

The first day went well, and I found it inspiring to see the group pushing themselves. Until, after six hours of kitesurfing, we returned to base salty, sunburnt, tired, but happy.

But the day hadn't finished. To the backdrop of a bright orange Sri Lankan sun, together with an obligatory rum and coke, we sat and watched video feedback of the days efforts.

It was hilarious! We laughed at each other's attempts at tricks on the water, gave encouragement and banter to progress made, and supported each other with tips. We were all at different levels but it didn't matter.

The week then settled into a routine of eat, sleep, kite and repeat and before I knew it, seven days passed, and it was over. The time had flown by. But it had been worth it. Not only had I met good people, as hoped, but the sense of progression had been motivating.

And, with the help of two of the group who were doctors, even my fractured toe had been manageable!

~ Checking in and writing ~

Once the coaching had finished, everyone returned to their daily lives and I was on my own again.

As the last person left, I also moved to a new camp at the far end of the Kapaladi village. I could still kitesurf from my location, but I wanted somewhere new to write from. It was time for a luxury treehouse on stilts, with a four-poster bed, and an outside shower carved from a coconut tree!

As I settled in to my new home for the next week, I discovered there was no wind forecast. This was unseasonal, but I didn't mind. I was ready to make an attempt at writing, my body needed a break from all the kitesurfing crashes, and

I'd picked up an infection in my foot that looked septic and needed a chance to heal.

And this was an incredible place to work from! I could see the Indian ocean on one side, coconut plantations on the other, and there were acrobatic yoga lessons available with a tantric yoga teacher called Nadine.

I found a quiet place to work, and made a start.

- - - - - - - - - - - -

At first, the writing went well, but progress was slower than I'd hoped. Whilst I recognised I'd left work to experience life and minimised most of my material belongings, turning my blog into a personal story was harder than I'd imagined.

However, I kept working for the next few days and drafted the start of my first chapter until, by the afternoon of the third day, as I was distracted by a voice, I decided it was time to take a break.

"Oi northerner, are you coming for a drink of rum? Don't forget it's your birthday today."

My birthday, I wondered, *it's not my birthday.*

Then I remembered.

Steve, the kitesurfing instructor who worked at the resort, who was calling me northerner even though he originated from York (much further north than Derby), had arranged with staff at the resort to bake me a cake.

It wasn't my birthday, he just wanted cake, but I was happy to take a break from writing and joined him for a drink.

That night, after a few glasses of rum, Steve got his wish. As we joined other guests to eat under a starlit Sri Lankan sky, the staff brought a cake out, and I was sang a round of happy birthday. I kept quiet, Steve ate the cake, and no-one was any the wiser.

It was fun, except Steve had told the staff I was forty-three and had this embossed on the side of the cake. Yet, not one person questioned it.

~ An adaptive plan ~

The next week passed as I continued with my attempt at writing and practised yoga. It was a relaxed time but by the seventh day I was ready to do something different.

Whilst I'd made progress with the first chapter of my book, there was still no wind predicted, and my visa was due to expire in twelve days.

So, I made a new plan.

I hired a motorbike and mapped a ride across the island which would give me a chance to see some of Sri Lanka and finished in the city of Colombo. From the city, I could extend my visa. Then, with more time, I would return here to kitesurf, keep working on my book, and then head back to the UK.

My motorbike was delivered to the resort the next day. I said goodbye to friends and promised to return in a few weeks. I then left the resort behind and navigated the sandy tracks that cut through the village until I picked up the main road.

I was heading one hundred and twenty kilometres east to my first planned stop of Anuradhapura, in the North Central Province, looking for fresh hopes and inspirations.

- - - - - - - - - - - -

After being in one place for over a week, I was happy to be moving again, but nervous for the roads. Not only were they crazy with traffic, the man who I'd hired the motorbike from had given me a helmet suitable for a skateboard, not a motorbike!

I reassured myself it was better than nothing, settled into the ride, and enjoyed the open road once again.

It didn't take long to pick up trouble.

An hour into the busy ride, two policemen who stood by the side of the road flagged me to stop. Thinking it the right thing to do, I did. They asked for my documents and when I showed them, they were not impressed. I had the wrong driving license, which meant I wasn't insured.

I did my best to contest an innocent mistake, but they confiscated my passport and wrote me an expensive fine. Things were not looking good until I mentioned the cultural tour I'd planned.

"You're Buddhist!" one of them exclaimed, gave me a huge grin and a curious wobble of his head. "Excellent."

"Errrr no," I replied, "but I'm interested in seeing your culture and religion and…."

He stopped me there. I seemed to have said enough. They ripped up my fine, handed me back my passport, and wished me a safe and pleasant trip. And somewhat bewildered at what had just happened, I was back on my way.

By late afternoon, I'd arrived at Anuradhapura. The town was crazy with traffic and people. Deciding it too much of a contrast to the sleepy village of Kapaladi I'd come from, I continued another twenty kilometres east to the smaller town of Mihintale.

Once I'd arrived, I knew this was the right choice. Mihintale seemed much more relaxed and, checking into a homestay, I decided that this area, known as the centre of the cultural triangle, was a perfect place to base myself for a few days.

~ Heading south ~

The next morning, I took a walk to explore the small town.

I first climbed Mihintale hill to see the Ambasthale Dagoba. This was the meeting place of Mahinde, son of an Indian emperor, and the King of Sri Lanka which led to the introducing of Buddhism to the country.

Once finished, I rode back to Anuradhapura to see the Jaya Sri Maha Bodhi fig tree – said to have come from a branch of the Sri Maha Bodhi in India, under which Buddha attained Enlightenment.

It was interesting to see, and busy with pilgrims offering food and flowers.

After returning to Mihintale and spending another night in the homestay, I decided to move on and rode south towards the city of Kandy.

To break up the one hundred and thirty kilometre journey, I stopped to climb the Pidurangala rock temple where I enjoyed a look over the wide plains of the Northern Province and the imposing Sigiriya rock.

I then continued to the busy town of Dambulla where I spent the night. But I wasn't impressed. The town, which was halfway between Mihintale and Kandy, was hot, dirty, and dusty, and my experience made worse when I became ill from the food I'd eaten that night.

The next morning, I left Dambulla early, promised myself to never eat spicy chicken Kotu again, and continued seventy kilometres south towards the mountainous interior of the island. Three hours later, I arrived at the city of Kandy as a tropical downpour of rain began. Within minutes, the roads flooded, and traffic came to a standstill.

It wasn't the best location to sit on a motorbike, so I parked, found shelter in a coffee shop, and spoke to the owner for recommendations of places to stay nearby. Thirty minutes later, once the rains had subsided and the water cleared, I followed directions to a recommendation and checked into a hostel that overlooked the mountains and the city

Once I'd settled in, I took a walk to explore.

Straight away, I found Kandy to be a nice place. It was easy, relaxed, and I suspected I would enjoy the civilisation if only for the quality coffee. But then I noticed something. I wasn't feeling my best.

At first, I put it down to the food I'd eaten in Dambulla which had made me ill. But now I wasn't convinced. I wasn't that happy, and I'd become lethargic with what I was doing.

~ Habituated with travel ~

The next day, I rode out of the city to explore the surrounding temples of Embekke Davale and Lankatilaka Vihara.

I felt better in the open space and wondered what had been wrong with me yesterday.

My itinerary had been tight, and I'd ridden a lot of kilometres on busy roads to get here, but I suspected my apathy was something else. Things seemed to lack lustre, and I wondered if I was riding around on my own, rushing to visit sights I wasn't bothered about seeing.

Then I realised it wasn't what I was doing, or seeing, to be the problem. It was me. I'd become travelled out. Things a year ago that may have been *wow, amazing, incredible*, didn't seem to inspire me. Until today I hadn't realised that was possible. On the positive side, recognising this gave me a kick to change my itinerary.

After my time at the temples, I left Kandy behind, made a conscious choice to slow down, and rode sixty kilometres south through the mountains towards Nuwere Eliya. This was the hill country and where the tea plantations grew. Perhaps not that special from a tourist point of view, but I hoped getting into the wilderness would pull me out of my slump.

The change worked. As I followed the mountain roads past different tea plantations, I felt better still, and realised I enjoyed the challenge of the ride and the open road, as much as the temples, restaurants, and people I met. And as I stopped at the small Alpine town of Nuwere Ellya and slept the night, I was happy to have adjusted my plans.

The next day, keen to keep the wilderness feel going, I continued south through the mountains to explore an area called Horton Plains National Park. It was a winding road, and an hour later I arrived at the entrance at a height of 2000 metres just as it started to rain. Typically, I didn't have a coat.

As I made my way in, I discovered the entrance fee to be fifty dollars. It was expensive, but I had no choice but to pay. I needed to cut through the national park to get to my planned destination of Ella, fifty kilometres from here, or I faced a four-hour detour!

Feeling frustrated, I paid the money and decided to explore the area whilst I was here, parked my motorbike, and began a hike to a vantage point known as World's End.

As I walked, I saw Buddhist monks dressed in traditional orange robes hiking, and a lot of other travellers. I soon forgot about the rain and the entrance fees and soaked in the mountain views and tropical feel of Sri Lanka's nature as the clouds lifted. Two hours later, I returned to my motorbike, happy to have stopped and, feeling like my old self again, continued on my way through the national park.

Late that afternoon, after riding isolated roads through forests and tiny villages, often having to cross slippery railway lines with no barrier crossings, I arrived at Ella - a small town and traveller's hub in the Uva Province known for its hills and cloud forests.

Once I got my bearings, I found a hotel recommended by a friend, negotiated a price, and checked into a room which overlooked a wide valley.

No parking was available for my motorbike, but with the manager's permission, I popped a wheelie into the lobby, kicked out my stand, and went to explore the small town.

~ Indecisions (and Google Maps) ~

For two days, I did little more than climb Ella hill and walk the famous Nine Arch railway bridge. The slowing down helped me catch up on sleep, but I was conscious of time, and I needed to decide what to do next.

With only three days left on my visa, should I ride two hundred kilometres to Colombo now, leaving myself plenty of time to get there. Or, should I ride one hundred kilometres in a different direction to explore a park famous for wild elephants called Uda Walawe? This would then mean a long and rushed ride to get to the city before my visa expired.

The next morning, I played it safe and chose the slow ride to the city.

The ride started well but then I changed my mind. Whilst here surely I should visit the elephant park! I found what I thought to be a shortcut to Uda Walawe using Google Maps on my phone and, assuming I could make up lost time, followed a dusty track which I was convinced would lead me straight there.

Two hours later, I was lost.

What had looked to be a direct route became a confusing and winding ride with lots of junctions. And because I'd expected it a short detour I'd not bothered to fill up on food, fuel, or water. With no choice but to continue, I kept going in the hope I would find civilisation.

An hour later, things got worse. I now had no water, and the day was getting hotter with the midday sun. My motorbike was also running on fumes. Then, just as I thought I may have to ditch my transport and walk, I saw a roadside coconut shack in the distance. I prayed there would be a village nearby.

I rode over with my motorbike sputtering, purchased a coconut from an old lady, drank it down, and asked her where I could buy petrol. She looked at me, smiled a toothless grin, but said nothing.

"Petrol?" I repeated, and tapped my motorbike, followed by "water?" and pointed to my mouth. I even tried "elephant?" to describe the park I was heading for and gave my best elephant impression.

This worked. She smiled again and pointed me toward a narrow road. I thanked her and, ten minutes later, after I'd climbed a hill with my motorbike gasping for fuel, I arrived at a village. I found a small shop that looked like a garage, stopped, and parked my motorbike.

As I waited, a man came out carrying petrol in a plastic container. He pointed to my tank, and I nodded my head.

As he poured petrol from the plastic container through a cooking sieve into my motorbike, I did my best to find out the way to the national park. He seemed sure in his suggestion of where I needed to go but spoke little English. With no choice but to try, I paid the man, started my motorbike, and rode.

An hour later, I'd found the elephant park. I was four hours later than if I'd come here first but, glad to have made it, I picked up a tour guide and began a mini safari. It was just what I'd hoped for.

Over the next few hours I had a fun trip with two guides. I saw herds of mating Pachyderms, hundreds of water buffalo, birds of prey, and crocodiles. All of this set to the backdrop of Horton Plains National Park where I'd hiked yesterday.

It was a good experience and worth the ride, but next time, I'll just go straight there.

~ Visas, motorbikes, and traffic ~

The following morning, I began the one hundred and seventy kilometre ride north-west to Colombo.

After two hours of riding, I'd made it as far as Ratnapura, still in the Sabaragamuwa Province, when the rear wheel of my motorbike locked up as I rounded a bend. The motorbike wobbled, kicked out, and for a second, I was certain I would end up in the path of oncoming traffic.

Once I'd regained control, I pulled over to look. The chain had jumped off the sprocket and jammed the wheel. But I had been lucky. It could have been much worse. Then, I noticed a repair garage across the street and, an hour later, certain I'd used up one of my nine lives, I was back on the road.

Late that day, I arrived at the busy city of Colombo and checked into a nice hotel. Then, I saw what a state I looked. My clothes, hands, and face were filthy from the days riding. The only clean area seemed to be around my eyes where I'd worn my sunglasses. But I didn't care. Once I'd got to my room, I dropped my bag and took full advantage of the hot shower, comfy bed, air-conditioning, and relaxed.

All I had to do now was extend my visa. This is what I'd come here for. I'd been told the process was easy, but to make sure I was at the office when it opened to avoid the queues. Otherwise, what was a one-hour job would take all day!

- - - - - - - - - - -

The following morning, I left the hotel at seven but as I walked out of the entrance, the man in reception stopped me and asked why I was up so early.

I explained my visa extension plan, but he smiled and wobbled his head. I was confused, and I asked him to explain.

"It's not possible to extend your visa today my friend."

"What?" I replied, thinking he was joking.

"Because the festival of Eid is today and all the government official buildings are shut."

I didn't want to believe him. This reminded me of that time in Tangier when the insurance office had been closed. So, I ignored what he'd said, left the hotel anyway, and arrived forty-five minutes later at the office, and waited.

An hour later, I returned to the hotel feeling foolish. He had been right, of course.

Instead of waiting around, I had another shower and decided to explore the colonial charm and modern chic of the city. And it was a pleasant surprise.

Once I'd got used to the horns blaring and tuk-tuks racing, I enjoyed exploring. The people were friendly, curious, and helpful, and I found it easy to spend an afternoon wandering the streets feeling like an ordinary tourist.

- - - - - - - - - - -

The next morning, I returned to the visa office and found the doors were open. It didn't take long to arrange a month's visa extension.

Once organised, I returned to my hotel, checked out, and began the one hundred and fifty kilometre ride north back towards the kitesurfing lagoons of Kapaladi. Then, I realised I'd left my sunglasses at a hairdresser I'd visited yesterday.

To collect them meant a ride through the centre of the city. I thought about leaving them but they were expensive glasses. So, I went for it and, two hours later, having navigated police check points, suicidal tuk-tuks, and racing buses, I'd got them back.

I then began the ride north to the kitesurfing camps.

As I rode and relaxed, I thought over my trip. It had been a rushed and interesting two weeks but also an indicator I was ready to focus on what I'd come to Sri Lanka to do. Which was kitesurf and try to write my book.

Then, as my thoughts distracted me, I rode onto the motorway with my motorbike. Since motorbikes weren't allowed on the motorway, and I didn't want another conversation with the police, I made a quick U-turn, re-found my way, and settled into my ride.

Four hours later, I was almost back to the kitesurfing area. The ride had been uneventful, and I was glad to be in a quieter part of the country. As I followed the road that took me close to my final destination of Kite Kuda, I was just thinking *how lucky I'd been to have had no accidents, considering how crazy the roads are,* when a lorry ahead of me lost control.

In what seemed like slow motion, he careered across the road and drove straight toward a family walking on a makeshift pavement. But then, somehow, with wheels skidding and bouncing on the concrete, he straightened up, regained control, and continued on his way as if nothing had happened.

The faces on the people said it all. They thought they would be hit. I wasn't sure what to think except *there but for the grace of God go I!*

~ The benefit of slow travel ~

Late that afternoon, I arrived at the village of Kapaladi and stopped at a small shop to pick up fruit.

A young girl who played with her family outside the entrance of the shop took a liking to me, threw her ball, and laughed as I kicked it back. She reminded me of my niece and nephew back home.

I did my best to entertain her before continuing back to Kite Kuda, where, for the first time in two weeks, I dropped my motorbike. Despite the fall, nothing was damaged except my pride, and I was glad to be back as familiar faces welcomed me and asked about my trip.

I told a few stories, drank a beer, and went to bed, tired after the full days riding. But, as I did, the manager asked how long I wished to stay.

"Just one week," I replied, certain that after a rest I would be ready to move onto another kitesurfing camp in the area. But I was wrong. Four weeks later, I was still there.

- - - - - - - - - - - -

It wasn't that I didn't want to move. In fact, I had every intention of going to explore other kite surfing camps in the area, but where I was had everything I needed.

There was a good crowd of people; a ten-minute walk to the kitesurfing location; and strong wind that blew almost every day. There were also acrobatic yoga lessons; sunny tropical weather; and no distraction other than deciding what trick to try for that morning or afternoon kitesurfing session. Except, of course, my idea to write a book.

Once I'd settled in and got back to the kitesurfing, it didn't take long to realise my kitesurfing skills had waned as I attempted a trick I could land three weeks ago and crashed hard on the beach.

This was frustrating. But after taking advice to "take the kiting easy," along with help from the talented locals and instructors that worked here, over the weeks I began again to make progress with my kitesurfing.

Staying in one place also gave me the chance to meet a host of interesting people as they passed through the camp.

There was a pilot from New Zealand keen on whiskey and evening conversation; a moon loving pole dancing hippy from Belgium with kitesurfing skills to put the boys to shame; and a retired soldier turned share dealer who'd been there so long, he'd become part of the furniture.

Whilst there, I also caught up with friends from the luxury resort I'd stayed in before my motorbike trip. This led to late night fires on the beach fuelled by the local alcoholic drink – Arrack; trips to offshore islands to kitesurf the flattest water I'd ever seen; and drunken evenings in the only restaurant in the village – a rustic pizzeria called the Kite House where the service was so slow, being drunk before you ate was guaranteed!

Then, before I knew it, my visa had expired, and it was time to leave. And, just like when I'd left Europe a year ago, and just like when I'd left South Africa six months ago, I wondered why I hadn't extended my stay for longer.

But I pushed the thought from my mind.

I'd come to Sri Lanka for a reason and enjoyed the coaching, progressed my kitesurfing, met good people, and even travelled. Whilst I'd made an effort with my writing, I'd not made as much progress as hoped, but this was OK. I now had a better appreciation of what was involved and this would be my focus once I was home.

So, after a final few drinks, I said goodbye to friends, took a taxi through all the madness of the traffic to the airport, and flew back to the UK.

Chapter 7
A New Focus

September 2016

*We can only do our work justice by examining what's possible and
deciding if we care enough to pursue it.*
Seth Godin - author and entrepreneur

~ Adjusting and focusing ~

From a tropical kitesurfing beach in Sri Lanka, to Heathrow
Airport and the London Underground in less than twelve
hours, was a reverse culture shock.

I kept telling myself *I didn't mind* as I battled through
people onto a train back to my parents' house. But when the
train stopped thirty miles from home and all passengers
disembarked in the rain to fight for a taxi because of a
collapsed bridge and blocked line, I couldn't help wonder *what
the hell am I doing here?*

But life wasn't all bad. I knew once I'd caught up with
friends and family, and adjusted back into the UK, things
would be OK. Of course I would miss the kitesurfing and
lifestyle of Sri Lanka. But I had my health and a clear idea of
what I wanted to do next – writing, supported by kitesurfing
and yoga to get the creative juices flowing.

- - - - - - - - - - - -

Within a few days of being back, and to help the transition
into Blighty, I made plans to visit the South Coast of the UK.
A friend had moved to the area to work and live and
discovered, in his words "an epic, secret kitesurfing spot."

He'd convinced a few friends, me included, to drive south and look. Before we even got there, I was apprehensive. I'd just spent two months in Sri Lanka. I doubted this would be that good.

It was a Saturday morning when myself and two kitesurfing mates made the drive south. As expected, my fears were confirmed after we'd arrived and found a large shallow pond of dirty looking water and rocks. It was much worse than I'd expected. Plus, we had driven two hundred miles to get here.

"What the hell is this place we've come to?" demanded Scooby, one of my mates, as we walked to investigate. We all agreed. It was not what we had been sold, and my friend came close to being outcast. But, unperplexed by our worries, he told us to "just relax and wait until the tide filled the area."

When it did, it transformed the now nicknamed 'dirt pond' into one of the best locations I have kitesurfed in the UK. It really was good. I had the chance to show off my new skills, my mate was forgiven, and a good time was had by all.

As friends returned to Derby late that evening, rather than rushing home, I stayed south and explored the coastline. And it was a relaxed time. I fished, kitesurfed at my new favourite beach, and spent time with a mate.

As a strategy to transition back into UK life, it worked and I ventured back to my parents' house a few days later for a family birthday feeling fresh, relaxed, and ready to focus on writing my book.

- - - - - - - - - - - -

Once I'd settled back into Derby, I made another start with my writing. However, despite my enthusiasm, a mental block kicked in!

I'm not sure why. I was convinced this was the right project for me, but the harder I tried, the more I forced, the less progress I made. Then, I became frustrated. Because there were plenty of other things to do instead – like get a job that paid money; go kitesurfing to a warm destination; perhaps even do some volunteer work.

I realised then I needed to make a decision, and I asked myself a question: *Did I care about what I wanted to do enough to focus on the one thing, even if it had no guarantee of success?* I told myself I did.

With that in mind, I estimated it would take me until the end of the year to finish my project. The month was September, and I believed that would be enough time. But I also wanted to base myself somewhere which would encourage me to work.

I had no need to stay in Derby and my main pull was back to the South Coast of the UK. I wanted somewhere I could sleep in my campervan, kitesurf, practice yoga, and of course, write.

Then, out of the blue, I received an email.

~ Serendipity ~

The email was from Yvonne, my yoga teacher and friend from Cape Town.

She didn't contact me often, but I'd asked her advice on practicing yoga. She'd replied, and suggested I follow a certain style of practice, and provided names of two reputable teachers in the UK. As was typical Yvonne, it also read, in no uncertain terms:

"If I was serious about practising yoga, I should stop faffing about and get on with it." That was her trademark style. Straight to the point and very encouraging.

Out of curiosity, I looked into her suggestions, but dismissed them as they were far from Derby. Then something curious happened. As I was researching studios to practice at on the South Coast, I discovered one teacher Yvonne had mentioned was running an intensive week of yoga – at the very studio I was looking at.

At first, I didn't think much of it. But, as Yvonne couldn't have known, I was looking at studios on the South Coast of the UK, plus the teacher she mentioned would be there but normally based four hundred miles away, I saw a coincidence.

I followed it up, discovered someone had cancelled and one space had become available. Then, something else happened that convinced me I was heading in the right direction.

Since returning from Sri Lanka, as well as writing, I'd been thinking about options for part-time work. Becoming a kitesurfing instructor seemed an obvious choice, but the one week training for the internationally recognised qualification never ran when I was free – until now, in the same area as the yoga course, one week later.

I made enquiries. Found out that this course only ran twice a year in this part of the country, and spaces were available.

"Am I being told something here?" I thought to myself. "Or is this just what happens when you free yourself up from restrictions and limitations?"

I wasn't sure. Either way, it was refreshing to find I didn't need to be halfway round the world for things to happen that supported a direction I wanted to follow. And, from my experience, when opportunities come up like this, it's best to see where they lead.

That evening, I gave it some thought, decided to go for it, packed my campervan, and got ready to move 'down south'. This time to the Purbeck peninsula.

~ Working for clarity ~

The following morning, I made the two hundred mile drive south. As soon as I arrived, I knew things would be good. It was a beautiful part of the country, easy to free camp, and the weather fine.

The yoga course began the day after I'd arrived and the week was great. Not only was it physically demanding, I met some nice people, experienced a new style of yoga practice, and found, similar to how I felt after running and meditating, yoga worked my body whilst giving a sense of clarity.

Once the yoga training had finished, I drove twenty miles east along the coast for the kitesurfing instructor training.

It was also good, and I enjoyed the fresh learning experience. However, before I could legally teach, I needed to complete a first aid course and, typically, the next available course was in Derby.

Accepting that would not happen quickly, I found a coffee shop to work from near a yoga studio and a beach, concentrated on my writing, and got to work.

- - - - - - - - - - - -

At last, I started to make progress. The campervan life, yoga, kitesurfing and minimal distraction worked, and in a week I drafted almost 10,000 words.

However, when I read back over my work, I still swung towards a story of travel and I wondered if I could give more thought to my experiences.

I knew there was no point worrying. I'd made a good start. So I took a break and returned to my parents' house in Derby for my Dads seventieth birthday. I also caught up with friends and completed the first aid course to finish my kitesurfing instructor training.

One week later, with a fresh mindset, and as a qualified kitesurfing instructor, I moved back down south. Once again, to the Purbeck peninsula and carried on with my writing.

The change had done me good.

Over the next few weeks as I worked from coffee shops, I made headway with my writing and I was happy with what I'd written.

Whilst in the area, I also picked up work as a freelance kitesurf instructor and explored other parts of the Jurassic Coast. I even met the TV presenter Julia Bradbury as she was filming the show Countryfile when I flirted with her camerawoman whilst out on a hike.

However, I was so distracted by her, I ended up leaving all my notes for my book in a pub overnight! Thankfully, I got them back the next day.

- - - - - - - - - - - -

The next month then passed quickly. My time had been productive, but as November came and the seasons changed, the opportunities to teach kitesurfing lessened.

It also turned dark early, and the weather became cold. And, as I slept in my campervan on the top of windswept cliffs and isolated carparks, I knew it wasn't the best approach to living. In fact, it was quite depressing. When I admitted to myself I'd stopped making progress with my writing and was now sitting in coffee shops pushing words around a page, I knew I had to make a choice. Did I put the writing on hold and do something new; or keep going with what I'd started?

I decided to stick with it. I'd made a good start, and I enjoyed the work. Plus, I was convinced there was a benefit to what I was doing. But, I also knew I would be better somewhere warm, windy, and with a strong yoga scene.

So, the next day I returned to Derby, locked my campervan up for the winter and, trusting my instinct, booked a flight to Cape Town.

Chapter 8
The Mother City

November 2016

If your life was a book, what would the title be?
Unknown

~ Making headway ~

A few days later, I flew into the Mother City.

I was happy to see Table Mountain and the Atlantic Seaboard from the sky again. It was the middle of November and I hoped to finish writing my book by the end of the year. My plan was to wrap up my story and fly back to the UK, send my manuscript to a publisher, and then drive to Italy for some snowboarding.

I felt so well organised, I even booked a return flight for the 31st of December.

Once I'd landed, I collected my hire car and drove straight to my accommodation. To give myself the best chance of success, I'd decided to base at a shared kite house close to one of the main beaches for kitesurfing.

It was a modern place run by a friend from the UK, complete with a transient mix of kitesurfers and windsurfers and a view of Table Mountain. Not only did I think I'd appreciate the company, when I got fed up with writing, I could walk five minutes to the beach, and go kitesurfing.

This, I knew, would be good.

- - - - - - - - - - - -

Once I'd settled into Cape Town and caught up with friends from my previous visit, I soon got into a routine.

Most days began at five-thirty am with a drive to a downtown yoga studio. Other guests thought I might be up to no good leaving the house, but practice started early and I wanted to beat a friend to the studio. Apparently, I brought a competitive edge to yoga!

I then practised yoga from six am to eight am and, once showered and changed, chose a coffee shop to sit in and write. It was a good start to my day and, once I'd finished writing, I returned to the shared kite house, ate lunch, and then went kitesurfing.

This was now my life.

- - - - - - - - - - - -

As the next month passed in the windy, sandy, haze of the city life, I had a good time and I was productive. But, as the end of December approached, I realised my idea to finish writing by the end of the year had been optimistic.

I needed more time, and I wondered what to do. I had the choice to stay here, but what about my plan to return to the UK and then drive to Italy? Despite having everything I needed here, for a moment I was torn.

But, after friends suggested I needed to put other plans on hold and get on with what I'd come here to do, I stayed.

They were right, of course. But it wasn't just writing I got on with.

I also stopped drinking alcohol, turned down most offers to late night parties, and focused on practising yoga. And, for a while at least, as I made progress, it was worth it.

~ This is Cape life ~

Time passed fast, the new year arrived, and I spent the evening at the shared kite house with a group of fun Scandinavians.

Since being in Cape Town, my kitesurfing had improved, and my yoga progressed. I also spent days on the beach, helped with a seal rescue, had an occasional evening in the city, and saw a baby humpback whale up close while snorkelling with seals!

Even though some days were more productive than others, my writing also flowed. But, having learnt lessons in the past from not over-focusing on what I was doing, at the start of the new year I broke my routine with a road trip to explore the Western Cape.

- - - - - - - - - - - -

The first place I visited was Panthera Africa – the sanctuary I'd volunteered at a year ago.

After contacting the owners, Liz and Cat, I made the one hundred and fifty kilometre drive through the Hottentots-Holland mountain range. It was cooler in the mountains than the city and the scenery kept me interested until, two hours later, I pulled up at the gate where they welcomed me with open arms.

It was great to see them again and I was amazed at how much had changed. As they showed me round, I recognised, in less than a year they'd built three new enclosures and homed two sterilised female lions.

"To keep the boys happy," they told me, laughing.

They were interested in my plans, gave me encouragement to keep writing, and took me to speak to Joseph who was hard at work building a fourth new enclosure. He was as happy as before. Still smiling and still laughing.

Whilst there, I also walked the grounds on my own hoping to see Achilles the lion and Arabelle the tiger. But they were hiding. Like most of the animals at the sanctuary, they were taking shelter from the midday sun.

I didn't have the chance to stay long at Panthera Africa, but happy to have visited, I vowed to return soon with a signed copy of my book.

- - - - - - - - - - - -

After the visit to the sanctuary, and a few days exploring the sea-side town of Hermanus, I drove an hour inland to Franschoek.

I knew this to be one of the oldest towns in the Republic of South Africa and I wanted to get a sense of the countries colonial history and sample the wines grown here.

After an evening in the small town I continued towards Stellenbosch – the second oldest European settlement in the province after Cape Town. I then spent a few days exploring the so called 'City of Oaks' that nestled in the mountainous nature reserve of Jonkershoek.

Once finished in the winelands, I returned to Cape Town, collected my friend Sally, and then drove three hundred kilometres north to the Cederberg mountains – named after the endangered tree endemic to the area.

Once we'd arrived, we found an isolated mountain hut full of spiders to sleep in and then spent days hiking, evenings cooking outdoors, and gazed at stars uninterrupted by any kind of light pollution. It was a fun time. The mountains are famous for dramatic rock formations and San rock art, and it was another interesting part of the Cape to explore.

After four days, because my friend Sally had to be back at work, we returned to the city happy with the mini adventure, and my life continued as before.

~ Getting feedback ~

As the end of January approached, I'd been in South Africa ten weeks. In that time, I'd climbed up Table Mountain five times; taught yoga classes on the beach to other kitesurfers; and become the longest staying guest at the shared kite house. Things were going well, so I extended my visa.

I had left my application late, but this didn't seem to be a problem. The immigration office advised it could take ten weeks for my new visa to come through and I wouldn't be able to leave the country without it, but I could think of far worse places to be stuck!

In the meantime, I sent my work for feedback. Until now, I'd kept my writing to myself and I thought it wise to get another opinion.

My only contact was a UK based author who had a Ph.D. in Happiness. He'd offered to look, so I emailed him my writing with my fingers crossed.

His feedback came back a few days later, positive and supportive, but also suggested "whilst it's an interesting story of travel, you could be more reflective."

I appreciated the comments and that night, while out with friends, I considered what he'd said. His feedback was motivating and encouraging. But I also knew it would mean more work.

Whilst that wasn't a problem, and I was happy living in Cape Town and this was another enjoyable experience, this was developing into more of a project than I'd ever imagined!

- - - - - - - - - - - -

A few days later, I decided to take a break from the city.

I wanted a chance to absorb the feedback and decide how to approach it. I knew of a small town called Greyton in the Overberg region, beyond the Hottentots-Holland mountain range. It was only two hours away and I suspected this would be a good place to base myself.

The following morning, I made the one hundred and fifty kilometre drive east. When I arrived, I found vernacular style houses, dusty streets, and a post box. There wasn't much here, but it had an old-world charm.

A friend had mentioned there was a farm on the outskirts of town with a choice of Indian style tipi or hobbit houses to sleep.

It sounded an interesting place, so I found the farm, chose a hobbit house for a week, and settled into my environment.

- - - - - - - - - - - -

At first, I wasn't sure how to handle the feedback, but I believed it was useful.

Of course, it was up to me how to take it but, because I'd wanted to be more reflective, I decided to spend the next few days looking over my work.

Sometimes this was enjoyable, mostly it was laborious, but this was where I became more earnest with my writing.

And, perhaps because more time had passed, or I was looking with a fresh mindset, but I started to appreciate some of what I'd experienced so far.

One thing of which was about life being a journey with few certainties.

I knew it a cliché, but it kept coming to mind because, when I'd left my job, I hadn't known if it was the right thing to do. In fact, many people hinted it was foolish to leave a well-paid career with a final salary pension scheme.

Yet, what I'd now realised was the more I'd embraced this uncertainty, the more I'd embraced the unknown, the better things had worked out.

I couldn't help but wonder if life is about embracing what you don't know and still giving it your best shot.

~ Time for a change ~

After one week in Greyton, I returned to Cape Town.

It had been a good break. The time away had motivated me to keep writing and life continued as before.

Over the next six weeks, I worked hard on my story in-between exploring the Atlantic Seaboard beaches on the western side of the Cape Peninsula. I also took in incomparable sunsets as I drove the picturesque Chapman's Peak Drive.

My visa extension was also accepted, I kept kitesurfing, and spent my birthday in a yoga studio organised by my friend Sally.

Then, it was suddenly April! I'd been in Cape Town almost five months. This was the longest I'd stayed in one place in two years and, without realising it, I'd put down roots.

But then something shifted.

It had been subtle at first, but my mood changed. The weather had become cold and cloudy; I injured my shoulder overstepping my yoga practice; and my writing stopped. Once again, I'd got stuck.

I explored options to loosen myself up – first living at a different kite house and then a friend's sofa. Whilst it worked for a while, I'd lost my focus and drive. Perhaps I'd concentrated too hard with my writing, but I'd hit the wall, and I needed a step change.

As I considered my options, I decided not to confuse myself with fresh experiences, and chose to return to the UK. I believed it the least disruptive way of finishing what I'd started.

It was now the middle of April, and I made a call to my parents to check it was OK for me to move back to their house.

"Hi dad."

"Hi John."

"I'm coming back to the UK, but I won't be there long. I'm wrapping up my book."

"How long's long?"

"A month, maybe two. I wanted to check it's OK to come home."

"Yes of course. See you soon."

So I booked a flight, said goodbye to friends, watched one last South African sunset, and flew back to the UK after five months of living in a different country.

Chapter 9
Finishing the Story

May 2017

Sometimes progress looks like a bunch of failures.
Unknown

~ A reality check ~

After putting down roots in Cape Town, adjusting back into the UK life proved difficult. And, just like when I'd returned from Europe, I crashed hard!

It wasn't surprising. Five months of sun-kissed-windswept-beaches of Cape Town to the industrial Midlands is quite a contrast. Even though I'd returned for a reason, at first, I struggled with the realisation of what that might be.

But, after one week in bed ill and another week moping around, friends messaged to say they were on holiday in North Wales and asked me to join them.

I was happy for the invite. This was a good excuse to go kitesurfing at my favourite beach, Rhosneigr, and I wanted to be close to the ocean to finish writing my book. After the efforts in Cape Town I was convinced it wouldn't take long, so I packed my campervan and drove west.

- - - - - - - - - - - -

My trip turned out to be a much-needed fun time.

I caught up with friends I'd not seen for years and had the chance to show off my kitesurfing and yoga skills – until I ripped my jeans and was politely asked to stop!

While there, I also took in sunset beach walks, kitesurfed waves that rolled in with the unsettled spring weather, and chilled out. It was great to be outdoors, and it was good to see friends.

After a few days of barbecues and beers, my friends returned to their daily lives and I stayed in Wales. Time at the beach had reinvigorated me and I felt motivated to wrap up my book project and make plans for another adventure.

I then spent a week drafting what I hoped was close to being my final story and emailed it for feedback. This time to my author contact along with family and friends.

I then drove back to my parents' house and, convinced that I'd almost finished writing, thought about publishing options and another adventure. I wasn't sure where yet, but South America held appeal, as did Europe in my campervan.

Then, a few days later, whilst sitting at my parents' house, I received my second round of feedback. It wasn't what I'd hoped and most people said something similar:

"I'd taken the life out of the story."

I had to laugh. With my recent efforts, I'd edited it to death!

~ A chance to live a life of travel and new experiences ~

At first, I hesitated to do any more work on my book.

I'd been back in the UK a month and I couldn't help but wonder if I was doing the right thing. I'd left work to free myself up, yet here I was working full time again – but this time for no money!

To take my mind off things, I fixed up my old motorbike stored at my parents' house. I recognised a distraction can sometimes give clarity on what to do and I enjoyed a few days of working with my hands.

Once done I made plans to take a ride on my motorbike and visit a friend I'd not seen for a year. I hoped a chat with a mate would give a new perspective on what I was trying to achieve.

That night, someone stole my motorbike.

I couldn't believe it.

The police recovered the motorbike a few days later, but it was beyond economical repair. Perhaps this was bad luck. Nothing had happened in five months of Cape Town and now this. Part of me wondered if I was being told something.

To cheer myself up, I remade my plans and decided to base myself in Norfolk on the east coast of the UK. A storm had been forecast and the kitesurfing looked like it had potential to be good. I also hoped a mix of campervan life and sports would motivate me to put the life back into the story!

With that in mind, I packed my campervan and drove one hundred and twenty miles east to the north Norfolk coast.

- - - - - - - - - - - -

Once I'd arrived at Norfolk, I quickly settled into campervan life and kitesurfing.

It wasn't as exciting as Cape Town, but I'd timed my visit with an unseasonal spring heatwave and met a half German, half Swedish girl called Andrea one evening when I introduced myself to her and her friends on a boat which had been converted into a bar.

I also found a good coffee shop to work from and, over the space of a few weeks, had some exciting kitesurfing sessions.

Perhaps it was the peace and quiet of Norfolk I'd needed all along. Or the company. Or the change of environment, but once again I enjoyed what I was doing, and the writing flowed. And, as I put life back into the story, I started to appreciate what the past two years had been about.

It was no more complicated than I'd given myself a chance to live a life of travel and new experiences, whilst working towards a simpler way of living. Which was great. It's what I'd wanted, and it was reassuring to know my efforts had been worth it.

But I also recognised something else.

Before I'd left my job, I'd been living my life on autopilot. Whilst there may have been nothing wrong with that, it's why I believed stepping out of my comfort zone had done me so much good!

~ Just a few Welsh benefits ~

After another three weeks of writing, kitesurfing, and topping up my tan in Norfolk, I returned to my parents' house and thought about what to do next.

My time away had been productive. I hadn't finished writing yet, but recent feedback from friends had been positive and I was back on the right track.

Then Andrea, my friend from Norfolk, contacted me and suggested we meet.

She was now living and working in South Wales. Even though it would mean moving again, it seemed a good plan. Not only did combining campervan life, kitesurfing, and writing work for me, South Wales was where I'd started to write a book.

This was a coincidence. Maybe I could finish where I'd started, so I arranged to meet her, packed my campervan, and made the two hundred mile drive south-west.

- - - - - - - - - - - -

I quickly settled into this remote part of the UK, caught up with my friend, and kept on with the writing.

Because my campervan had become my workspace, my office was a choice of different beach coves along the Pembrokeshire coast. One day, I worked from a village called Trefin, the next Abercastle, and the next Abereiddy.

Whilst I was working like this, people who saw me often commented how lucky I was. I knew I wasn't earning any money, but it got me wondering what might be possible for the future.

It was during those quiet beach days, between walking across cliff tops, kitesurfing, and exploring Welsh pubs with my friend, that I thought of the benefits the past few years of travel and adventure had brought. It seemed a good way to conclude my story.

There were many, but what stood out was the satisfaction of having done what I'd wanted. I'd found myself, or perhaps put myself, in strange and unfamiliar situations and come out better for the experience. Even if it hadn't been that nice all the time.

Because of this, I'd also been given a fresh perspective and had to adapt to different situations and people, which meant the travel and change had broadened my horizons a little.

And who knows where this could lead?

Perhaps a new career or relationship; or the confidence to travel to a new country to experience a different culture; even just appreciating what is sometimes right in front of you.

- - - - - - - - - - - -

Two weeks later, my friend moved to another part of the UK.

She was short-term volunteering and had to go where the opportunity for work was. I stayed in the Pembrokeshire area but moved to free camp on a remote beach called Freshwater West.

An unseasonal storm had been forecast and, in-between writing, I wanted to see what weather it would bring. I hoped for strong winds and good kitesurfing conditions, and I hoped for one final session before I returned to Derby. It seemed an opportune way to end my time in Wales on a high.

Three days later, I got my wish.

When the forecast storm hit, it bought strong wind and rain. It was wild, exciting, and unpleasant to everyone else on the beach, but these are the real days of kitesurfing in the UK.

Once the conditions had settled, I walked to the water to set up my equipment. I knew I was in for an exciting session. The wind was still strong and froth from the ocean blew up the beach and mixed with swirls of sand intent on getting in my eyes.

There were two people on the water already. As I set up my equipment, one of them landed his kite, ran over, and checked I knew what I was doing.

"It's fucking wild out there mate," he shouted over the wind. "Are you sure you want to go for it?"

"Yes, definitely," I shouted back, just as a gust of wind knocked him off his feet.

Once I was ready to get into the water, I asked him to help launch my kite. He looked at me with concern but put my kite into position. I gave him the thumbs up and he let go.

Within an instant, the powerful kite was flying and snatching in the gusty conditions, trying to drag me across the beach toward some jagged rocks.

"You OK mate?" he shouted with panic in his voice as the kite pulled me straight past him.

But then he smiled. He must have seen the massive grin on my face.

~ The journey's end ~

It was the middle of August when I left South Wales. I'd been away for five weeks, but, because it was my mum's seventieth birthday, I was heading back to Derby.

My time in Wales had been worthwhile. Not only to see my friend and explore another beautiful part of the UK but I was sure I'd concluded my story. And, according to recent feedback from family, friends, and my author contact, kept the life in it!

On route home, I detoured and stopped at the beach where I'd surprised my parents a year ago after I'd returned from South Africa travelling.

Whilst South Wales had been where I'd decided to write a book, I realised this beach in mid-Wales was where I'd first come up with the idea. Once I'd arrived, I didn't stay long. Just long enough to walk the beach, run up a large hill that overlooked a wide bay, and get a strange sense of closure.

Three hours later, I was back in Derby.

- - - - - - - - - - - -

Over the next month, I kept busy with family birthday celebrations, got back to my yoga practice, caught up with friends, and wrapped up the final parts of my story.

Whilst I was surprised at how long this project had taken, I knew it had been worth it. I'd wanted to capture my experience and make sense out of my journey, and I was glad I'd seen it through to the end. Even if it had proven more of a marathon than a sprint!

All I had to do now was think about publishing. And I decided not to do that sitting in Derby.

Because I'd only visited my favourite beach in the UK once this year, I packed my campervan, and drove west to Rhosneigr, on the Isle of Anglesey. Right back to where this began two-and-a-half years ago.

- - - - - - - - - - - -

I settled straight into life in North Wales with one intention in mind – send my work out to as many publishers and agents as possible.

Things got off to a good start. I slept and worked from a friend's house and, to help keep clear-headed, walked to the beach or went kitesurfing in-between preparing my manuscript to send.

However, I soon found that each publisher or agent wanted to see something slightly different and, by the time I'd submitted my work to thirty-five different potentials, none that came with any guarantee of success, I stopped, and decided if nothing came from it, I would self-publish instead.

I then decided to drive to Snowdonia National Park to climb Mount Snowdon.

I was ready for a break from sending my work out and, because this was one of the first fun things I'd done after leaving my job, it seemed opportune for me to retrace my steps.

- - - - - - - - - - - -

It was Monday morning in the middle of October when I made the forty-five minute drive from Rhosneigr to the Snowdonia National Park.

The air felt cool; the sky was clear; and the sun was shining. I was on my own but I didn't mind. I arrived at the national park, parked my van, and made my way up to the summit.

As I walked, I couldn't help but smile. This was still living the way I wanted. Outdoors and free. At least for now. Two hours later, I stood at the top of the mountain. It had been a good hike and I'd walked fast to get here.

After a coffee and an obligatory summit photo, I walked back to my van and thought about what to do next. Since I'd finished writing and sent my work out to prospective publishers and agents, perhaps it was time to plan that next adventure.

However, an hour and a half later, once back at my van, my phone beeped to say I'd received an email. It was from a kitesurfing friend who was a team manager for one of the biggest kitesurfing brands. He was also a regular kitesurfer at Rhosneigr.

The email read "John, are you in North Wales, and have you seen the weather forecast? There's a storm predicted that's bringing gale force winds and a huge swell to western parts of the UK."

I had seen the forecast. It had been named 'Storm Brian' and was set on a clear path to hit the Welsh coast this coming weekend. It was the second storm to hit the UK this October, and I doubted many would be out kitesurfing in the conditions.

The email continued.

"If you're still around, Nick Jacobsen is flying in from America for the weekend. He wants to beat his current world record for the highest jump by a kitesurfer and will attempt it at Rhosneigr. It's a small window of opportunity but we'll do some filming and a photo shoot. You should come and check it out."

This was too good an opportunity to miss. I didn't know Nick personally, but he's well known in the kitesurfing community. Not just because he holds the world record for the highest jump with a kite.

Earlier in the year, as part of a Mercedes commercial, he'd jumped from the helicopter pad of the world's third highest building – the Burf al-Arab in Dubai, and used a kitesurfing kite to glide back down. And this was only one of his many crazy kite-related stunts!

With that in mind, I pushed thoughts of other adventures to the back of my mind, left Snowdonia National Park, and drove straight back to Rhosneigr.

And as I did, I couldn't help but wonder if this could be the start of my next book.

Afterword

Having received rejections from most of the publishers and agents whom I'd sent my work to, I put other adventure plans on hold and followed the self-publishing route.

One of the main benefits of going with a publisher was to get professional editorial support. Since this was no longer an option, with the help of family and friends, I did the work myself.

Whilst this meant I wasn't ready to publish until March 2018, it turned out to be a good thing.

The editing process encouraged me to weigh up my experiences and realise I'd found what I'd hoped for at the start of this journey – real benefit in taking a break, getting out of my comfort zone, and experiencing life in a different way.

I hope you have seen that throughout this story, and perhaps even recognised yourself within some of these words.

Printed in Great Britain
by Amazon